The Buddhist Religion

THE RELIGIOUS LIFE OF MAN
Frederick J. Streng, Series Editor

Understanding Religious Man
Frederick J. Streng

The House of Islam
Kenneth Cragg

Japanese Religion: Unity and Diversity
H. Byron Earhart

Chinese Religion: An Introduction
Laurence G. Thompson

The Buddhist Religion
Richard H. Robinson

The Way of Torah: An Introduction to Judaism
Jacob Neusner

The Hindu Religious Tradition
Thomas J. Hopkins

forthcoming:

Primitive Religions
Charles H. Long

The Buddhist Religion
A Historical Introduction

RICHARD H. ROBINSON
Department of Indian Studies,
University of Wisconsin

DICKENSON PUBLISHING COMPANY, INC.
Belmont, California

To Sita and Neil,
my daughter and my son,
kuladuhitre ca kulaputrāya

My gratitude goes to Fred Streng, who has proven as good an editor as he is a friend; to Mary Fujimoto and Dennis Lishka for typing the manuscript; and to Hanna Robinson for preparing the index.

L. C. Cat. Card No.: 79-103033

Printed in the United States of America

4 5 6 7 8 9 10

Table of Contents

Foreword

The Religious Life of Man series is intended as an introduction to a large, complex field of inquiry—man's religious experience. It seeks to present the depth and richness of religious concepts, forms of worship, spiritual practices, and social institutions found in the major religious traditions throughout the world.

As a specialist in the language and culture in which a religion is found, each author is able to illuminate the meanings of a religious perspective and practice as other human beings have experienced it. To communicate this meaning to readers who have had no special training in these cultures and religions, the authors have attempted to provide clear, nontechnical descriptions and interpretations of religious life.

Different interpretive approaches have been used, depending upon the nature of the religious data; some religious expressions, for instance, lend themselves more to developmental, others more to topical studies. But this lack of a single interpretation may itself be instructive, for the experiences and practices regarded as religious in one culture may not be the most important in another.

The Religious Life of Man is concerned with, on the one hand, the variety of religious expressions found in different traditions and, on the other, the similarities in the structures of religious life. The various forms are interpreted in terms of their cultural context and historical continuity, demonstrating both the diverse expressions and commonalities of religious traditions. Besides the single volumes on different religions, the series offers a core book on the study of religious meaning, which describes different study approaches and examines several modes and structures of religious awareness. In addition, each book presents a list of materials for further reading, including translations of religious texts and detailed examinations of specific topics.

We hope the reader will find these volumes "introductory" in the most significant sense: an introduction to a new perspective for understanding himself and others.

Frederick J. Streng
Series Editor

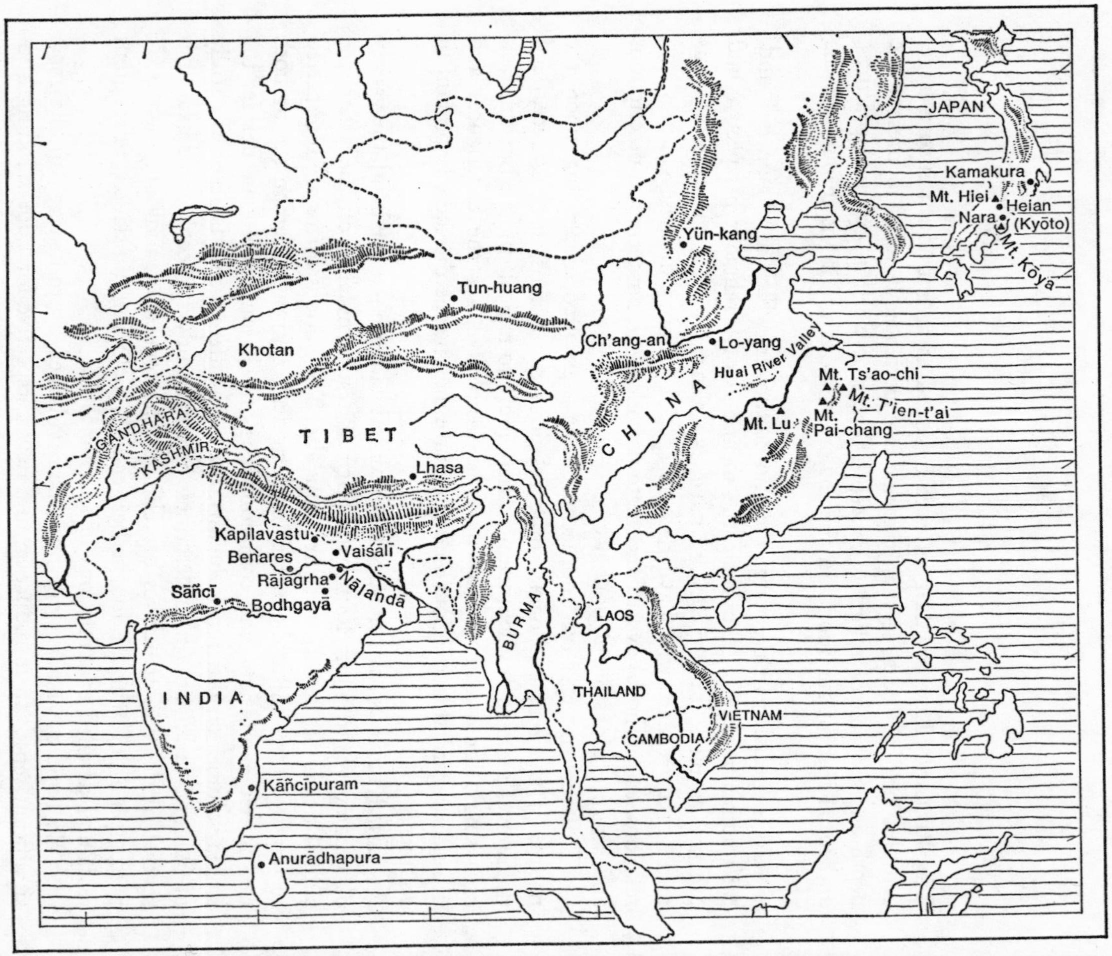
JAPAN
Kamakura
Mt. Hiei
Heian
Nara
(Kyōto)
Mt. Kōya
Yün-kang
Tun-huang
Ch'ang-an
Lo-yang
Huai River Valley
Mt. Ts'ao-chi
Mt. T'ien-t'ai
Mt. Lu
Mt. Pai-chang
CHINA
Khotan
TIBET
GANDHARA
KASHMIR
Lhasa
Kapilavastu
Vaiśālī
Benares
Rājagṛha
Nālandā
Sāñcī
Bodhgayā
BURMA
LAOS
THAILAND
VIETNAM
CAMBODIA
INDIA
Kāñcīpuram
Anurādhapura

1. The Scene Today

India

Bodhgayā lies seven miles from the Hindu holy city of Gayā, a railway point in the backward central area of Bihar State. The tourist-pilgrim who goes by cycle rickshaw emerges from the crumbling old city, past lotus ponds and tall palms, away from the little mountains that crop out of the plain, and along the sandy flats of the Phalgu River. The road passes shrines to obscure folk deities, mud-and-thatch huts, then a dusty little one-street bazaar. The rickshaw stops at the top of a slight rise. The visitor walks a few yards to the Mahā Bodhi Temple, the hundred-and-seventy-foot spire of which has held his gaze for the last mile. The four-sided tapering stone tower is substantially the same as when the Chinese pilgrim Hsüan-tsang saw it in 635 A.D. It was renovated in the eleventh century in the last period of splendor that Buddhism enjoyed in Eastern India before the cataclysmic onslaught of the Muslims about 1200 A.D. In its heyday, this holy place was visited by pilgrims from Ceylon, Indonesia, Tibet, and China. For over fifteen hundred years kings of India offered worship and donations here, and left their traces in sculptured stone.

This is the site where about 530 B.C. Gautama Siddhārtha Śākya attained supreme, perfect enlightenment and became a Buddha.[1] The event is as central and as momentous for Buddhism as the Resurrection is for Christianity, and equally fraught with mystery. Devout Buddhists aspire to attain that liberation from transmigration which Gautama declared he achieved while sitting on the "Diamond Seat" under the Bodhi Tree. Every event in the legend of the Enlightenment (*Bodhi*) is associated with some spot on this site, and ancient donors erected a monument on each, as if seeking to render perceptible the presence that had once graced the spot.

[1] All Indic words and names are given in Sanskrit rather than Pali so that the beginning student will not have to learn two forms for each term. Many words are identical in the two languages, e.g., *asura, Bodhi, Buddha, deva, Māra, nāga, Piṭaka, Rāhula, samādhi, Saṅgha, Sujātā, Tathāgata, Vinaya.* Common Sanskrit-Pali correspondences: *Abhidharma–Abhidhamma, Ārāḍa Kālāma–Āḷāra Kālāma, arhant–arahant, bhikṣu–bhikkhu, bodhisattva–bodhisatta, dharma–dhamma, dhyāna–jhāna, gandharva–gandhabba, Gautama–Gotama, Kauṇḍinya–Koṇḍañña, Kuśinagara–Kusinārā, maitrī–mettā, Maitreya–Metteya, nirvāṇa–nibbāna, prajñā–paññā, preta–peta, Śakra–Sakka, Siddhārtha–Siddhattha, skandha–khandha, śramaṇa–samaṇa, sthavira–thera, Sūtra–Sutta, Udraka Rāmaputra–Uddaka Rāmaputta, vijñāna–viññāna, yakṣa–yakkha.* Sanskrit /*ś*/ and /*ṣ*/ become Pali /*s*/, e.g., *Aśoka–Asoka, Tuṣita–Tusita.*

Hindu boys at the gateway to the main shrine sell rosaries made of Bodhi Tree nuts. The pippal tree is widespread in South Asia, but Buddhists offer special reverence to progeny of *the* tree. The one now growing at Bodhgayā is a descendant of the tree under which Gautama sat.

Ceylon

Anurādhapura, capital of Ceylon from the fifth century B.C. till the ninth A.D., is now a city of resplendent ruins. It lies among vast artificial irrigation lakes in the now sparsely populated plain of northern Ceylon. When seen from the peak of Mahintale, eight miles to the east, white domes of *stūpas* ("reliquary mounds") glimmer along the jungle skyline against the sunset. But Anurādhapura, though in ruins, is far from deserted. It is only 125 miles by rail from Colombo, and in February, 1966, the prime minister and the entire cabinet went by special train to celebrate the installation of a golden railing around the venerable Bodhi Tree said to be a slip brought in the third century B.C. from the one at Bodhgayā.

The Sinhalese philosophy professor takes his two young daughters and the Western visitor in through the outer wall and up to the inner complex surrounding the Bodhi Tree. (Buddhist shrines, unlike Hindu ones, are open to people of all nations and creeds.) There all four take lotus buds, fold the petals back, and place the flower offerings on a marble niche. The tree's branches are visible above the golden railing, which surmounts a high protective wall. The small chapel just to the left is quite ordinary. The interest of the shrine is not art but the hedged-in, pampered tree, revered as if through some speechless mode it could communicate the gist of the wonder that its parent witnessed.

Over lunch, the professor had been discussing scientific evidence for rebirth. Trained in England, he esteems the principle of verification as highly as any other analytic positivist. A Buddhist by tradition and conviction, he insists that the testimony of paranormal experience be seriously considered.

In Colombo, a high-ranking civil servant invites the visitor to a ceremony on the thirteenth anniversary of his father-in-law's death. The host's home is crowded with lay guests seated on mats. Eighteen saffron-robed monks file in, the host meeting each one and washing his feet at the door. The monks are seated, and the ladies of the house present them with gifts—towels, pillowcases, books—and serve them dinner. Monks of the Theravāda sect do not eat after midday, but this generous meal of rice, fish, vegetables, and fruit is adequate to last until next morning. The senior monk leads the laity in reciting the Three Refuges and the Five Precepts (see pp. 31, 48–49). Then he delivers a short sermon in memory of the deceased, stressing that we live on through our children, that how we bring up our family decides what kind of moral legacy we leave. Then he chants the scripture for offerings to the departed, while the hostess and her mother pour water offerings from a pot into a bowl. After this ceremony, the monks take leave, and the laity eat.

At the ancient and sizable shrine of Kelaniya, outside Colombo, murals in the central chapel show Mahinda, Aśoka's son, bringing Buddhism to Ceylon, and Portuguese soldiers desecrating and destroying the Kelaniya Temple. A gilded image of the Buddha seated in meditation posture occupies the shrine chamber of the main chapel. The side chapel contains a huge Reclining Buddha image, before which crowds of women and children offer flowers. An adjacent building holds images of Hindu gods before which Buddhist worshippers pray for mundane favors. In the spacious courtyard stands a huge, magnificent old Bodhi Tree.

The meditation center at Kanduboda, almost an hour's drive from Colombo, is devoted to practicing the controversial "Burmese method." The visitors walk around the men's meditation building (there is another for women), and observe that the four-by-eight cells are rather depressing, and afford little auditory privacy. The monk in charge receives the visitors kindly in his cabin, offers them milk from a green coconut, and invites questions.

"Is this method successful?"

"Yes, look at the testimonials in the visitors' book."

The visitors scan the book. A Dutch hitchhiker says that he attained *samādhi* ("trance of concentration").

"Is it necessary to attain the trances to achieve insight?"

"One passes quickly through the trances but does not stay in them."

Afterward, the two Sinhalese tell the Westerner that this sounds dubious. This method of cultivating insight apart from the trances has been denounced as heterodox by some of the most learned monks in Ceylon.

Tibet-in-India

The fourteenth Dalai Lama, legitimate spiritual and temporal ruler of Tibet, lives in exile in a mansion looking out over the lower hills toward the Punjab plains. The visitors climb fifteen minutes from the refugee-crowded bazaar of Upper Dharmaśāla, register with the Indian government checkpost just inside the barbwire fence, wait a few minutes in a well-carpeted and well-decorated room, and then are ushered into an ordinary-size sitting room where the Dalai Lama greets them with no more ceremony than a handshake. He is a tall, well-built man in his early thirties, with strong features, mobile expressions, and an aura of intelligence and sincerity unexpected in such an object of piety. The visitors have said they want to discuss Mādhyamika philosophy (see p. 54) with him. He asks, "Is this coffee table real?"

"From the relative standpoint, yes. From the absolute standpoint, no."

"But don't you perceive it?"

"Yes, but what we perceive is not what it seems to be."

After the visitor has undergone this examination, he asks: "Does one need to have cultivated insight through the meditative trances in order to understand Mādhyamika?"

The Dalai Lama says: "There is a lower degree of understanding that non-saints can attain, and then there is a higher degree accessible only to accomplished contemplatives." He goes on to ask the visitors whether they think the doctrine of rebirth can be scientifically demonstrated. If so, this would compel even such materialists as the Communists to acknowledge the reality of the spiritual realm. In the light of this knowledge, worldly contention would cease and larger nations would allow smaller nations to be free.

At Dalhousie, farther east in the Punjab hills, the lamas of a Tibetan craft community are preparing for ritual dances to celebrate the festival of Guru Rimpoche (Padma-sambhava, see p. 110), the legendary founder of Tibetan Buddhism. A procession of maroon-robed lamas walks around the ritual area, installing a multicolored picture of the appropriate Great King (see p. 24) at each of the four directions. This is the first of many measures to protect the dance from demons.

Later, a *maṇḍala* ("sacred diagram") with the divinities in their residences painted meticulously in colored sand is placed in the middle of the space within a large tent, and on top of the maṇḍala is set an altar table carrying several tiers of offering figurines modeled out of dough and brightly colored; two bowls containing, respectively, "long-life" pills and "long-life" water; an incense burner; and several large and splendid goblet-shaped silver butter lamps. Lamas come in, wearing their finest robes and large, mitre-shaped red hats. They recite their worship service before the altar, and then go out.

As the dance proper begins, four lamas enter in sorcerers' costumes, with large-brimmed black hats and robes of heavy, bright-hued brocades. They dance in a ring around the stage-ground, planting ceremonial daggers at the corners, and gradually increasing their tempo until, as the robes fly out and the booted feet kick higher, the dance reaches a climax. When the stage has been purified in this way of evil forces, two long-haired yogins come out wearing large, brightly painted masks. They jump in the air, cross their legs in "lotus" position, and land cross-legged on the ground. Their presence shows the scene to be a cemetery, a favorite place for ascetics to meditate. Then Guru Rimpoche comes on stage, followed by his eight transformations, alias-forms that he is said to have been able to assume magically. The "real" Guru Rimpoche sits on a high seat, while his aliases, all wearing striking masks and gorgeous costumes made in this craft community, go through solo dances which do not tell a story but simply express the character of each personality. The performance is accompanied by a weird orchestra of trumpets, oboes, cymbals, and drums. The dances are at once a magical rite and a contemplative exercise. Ideally, each actor is supposed to concentrate on his role until he "becomes" it.[2]

[2] I am obliged to Stephan V. Bever for showing me his excellent and detailed color slides and for explaining this Tibetan ritual dance. The craft community has now moved to Palampur, Himachal Pradesh. This particular dance is held in early July.

Vietnam

When the visitor lies awake before dawn in a guest room in the Xa Loi Pagoda, Saigon, the night-long noise of planes and helicopters is intermittently broken by distant explosions or drowned by the roar of army trucks along the treelined avenues. He dresses, hurries the few paces to the chapel, slips off his sandals, and squats on the colorful tiled floor just as an elderly monk begins to chant the first service of the day. The fast, fluting plainsong is punctuated occasionally with gong strokes. The monk alternately stands and kneels before a giant image of Gautama Buddha, and is half hidden by a wide offering table lacquered with scenes in the distinctive Vietnamese style. The image is at once impressive and attractive, serene in manner, modern and international in its facial expression. After the service, the visitor walks around to the alcove behind the image, where tables on either side hold rows of wooden memorial tablets inscribed with the Chinese "dharma-names" of the deceased. In the center, back to back with the large image, are photographs of the martyrs, the monks who underwent self-immolation during 1963 in the Buddhist struggle against the dictator Ngo-Dinh Diem. These photos, like the paintings of the martyrs found in all the modern Saigon temples, are stark and jarring.

On Sunday morning the Xa Loi chapel is crowded with laymen participating in the chief congregational service of the week. They kneel and bow in rows on the bare floor, chanting responses from little manuals in roman-letter Vietnamese, men sitting to the left of the center aisle and women to the right. There are four or five uniformed Americans in the congregation. Two weeks later, one of them marries a Vietnamese girl in a Buddhist ceremony.

The Xa Loi temple has a good library of Buddhist books in Vietnamese, Chinese, French, and English. It and the classroom downstairs are used by the Buddhist University, pending completion of the new building. Fifty students come to hear the foreign speaker, and the chairman later apologizes for the small crowd. Only three months have passed since the Buddhist demonstrations were quelled by the government; dozens of youth leaders are still in jail, and many others are prudently avoiding public meetings. The talk is followed by a twilight dinner party in the temple garden. After the meal a singsong, featuring solo and group renditions of folk and popular songs, is held by lamplight in the temple portico. Boys and girls tease each other and laugh. The atmosphere is the worldwide one of the church social.

The elderly layman sits in the guest's room at the pagoda and discusses the state of Buddhism in Vietnam. The true Buddhist, he says in French, should be a nirvāṇa-seeker rather than a political activist. Without religious depth, such movements as the current one will wither away and leave Buddhism no better than before. The aim of the Buddhist Study Association, of which the speaker is president, has been to focus attention on the study of the scriptures and to encourage the individual layman to lead a good Buddhist life. But Vietnamese Buddhism is rent by jealousies and contention. The monks grudge influence to the laity, and even among the monks themselves there is discord between the modernizers and the traditionalists.

The car stops near the tombs of the former abbots of a Zen monastery on the outskirts of Saigon. The visitors meet the present abbot, an elderly ascetic in dark robes who shows them first into the central corridor where portraits of his predecessors are arrayed in shrines. To the right is a large hall where the forty-eight monks eat, and sleep on long hardwood benches with only thin mats for bedding. The chapel, to the left, is small, dark, and crowded with images. Unlike the Xa Loi Pagoda, it is not a place for congregational worship. Along one wall are the ten judges of hell, a favorite Far Eastern cult set. The images in the central shrine are darkened with age. The temple is three hundred years old, it is said. Elegant Chinese inscriptions adorn the wooden pillars.

As the car approaches the crossroads in front of the Cambodian Embassy, the young highschool teacher says that this is where Thich Quang-duc performed self-immolation in June, 1963. The seventy-three-year-old monk sat down on the pavement while an attendant poured gasoline over him. Then he lit a match, ignited himself, and burned to death with serene composure, evidently in a meditative trance. The visitor asks his guide what his reactions were at the time. First shock and horror. Then realization of the gulf between true selfless devotion and his own lukewarm commitment to Buddhism. Then pride that there were such men in Buddhism today. Some subsequent self-immolators, he says, were cranks seeking notoriety. But Quang-duc was a pure-minded saint.

Japan

The young Japanese scholar and his Western guest pay the entrance fee (usual at famous old Japanese temples), take off their shoes, and shuffle along the plank corridors to look at the sixteenth-century rock garden for which this temple is famed. Rocks and pieces of wood artfully lure the viewer's concentration. Before long, one becomes quieter imperceptibly, stops having associative fancies, and enjoys this microlandscape as a world in its own right. The visitor is mildly jolted when a robust, fortyish Zen monk in light-colored robes, with shaven head, quicksilver facial expression, and glowing eyes bounces in and offers to explain the garden.

"What is there to explain?"

"Well, nothing, but I have an explanation that I've made up for the tourists."

"Doesn't the garden explain itself?"

"Yes, it does. You speak Japanese extraordinarily well."

(This being outrageously false.) "You are flattering me." (A bass giggle, then the mischievous silence of the saints.)

After a few minutes of jocular sparring, the monk invites the two sightseers to join him for tea in a nearby room. There he starts talking straight and asks about the situation in Vietnam.

The young scholar tells the visitor afterward that the monk is the director of the University of Kyōto Zen Club. He has finished his Zen training and is a master. The Zen Club practices meditation regularly, and sometimes holds retreats. As they go to a restaurant, the guide admits to the visitor that he finds meditation a refreshing respite from the grueling study of Sanskrit and Tibetan scholastic treatises. Unlike many Buddhologists, he is not the son of a priest. He took to studying Buddhism in quest of a viable philosophy of life, an alternative to the facile hedonism now dominant in Japan. What has he found in Buddhist studies? It is hard to say, but he is still young, still looking, and well on his way to a noteworthy academic career.

At Tōji (the Eastern temple) south of Kyōto Station, old women in mushroom-shaped peasant hats circumambulate the statue of Kōbō Daishi (p. 102), who founded the temple in 823. They pick up and put down tally sticks at the end of each round, and mumble formulas as they walk. They are seeking relief from physical ailments.

Fifty miles south, in the precincts of Kōyasan Monastery, which he founded in 816, Kōbō Daishi's remains are enshrined at the end of a long mortuary glade lined with cedars, cypresses, and the illustrious dead of intervening centuries—saints and generals, emperors and poets. One plot is reserved for ashes of employees of the Osaka Life Insurance Company. Bands of aged pilgrims clutching their rosaries in bare hands struggle through the snow, reciting their offices at each station on their route. The visitor asks the student monk who accompanies him: "Have you practiced meditation?"

"Yes, I did a session of a couple months last year."

"What did you get out of it?"

"Nothing much."

"Did you enjoy it?"

"No."

"Then why did you do it?"

"Because our sect [Shingon] requires it as part of our training. I am going to take over the temple when my father retires.

A high gateway and a simple wooden signboard mark the entrance to the little Jōdoshinshū Temple (see p. 103) in a back street of Kyōto. Inside, the "minister's" family's quarters are on the left, and the small chapel is straight ahead across the courtyard. The congregation leave their shoes on the veranda, go in, and squat on the mat-covered floor. A large part of the chapel is taken up by the shrine, gilded and lacquered and hung with ornaments under an over-all canopy. The central object in the shrine is a very old and beautiful statue of Amida Buddha (see p. 66). He is standing on a lotus, his right hand raised in the gesture of reassurance and his left hand outstretched, palm upward, in the gesture of gift granting. A halo rises behind his head. On each side of the Buddha-image is a scroll-painting, one of Shinran (the sect's founder), and the other of Hōnen, Shinran's teacher (see p. 103).

On New Year's morning, fifty or sixty people have gathered for the first public service of the year. Following the lead of the minister, they chant the

Three Refuges in classical Japanese, then recite the Profession of Faith: "Forsaking all sundry practices and attitudes of self-power, we rely wholeheartedly upon Amida Buddha for salvation in the life to come. . . ." Then the congregation chants Shinran's "Hymn of Right Faith," a long poem in Chinese giving the history of the Pure Land teaching. The melody is involuted, the tempo is slow, and the effect is solemn and compelling. Afterward, they chant a stanza dedicating the merit (from reciting the hymn) to all sentient beings so that they may attain rebirth in Amida's Pure Land. The minister then delivers a short sermon. The service concludes with everyone reciting "Salutation to Amida Buddha."

An official of the Risshō Kōseikai ("Society for Establishing the Right and Co-operative Self-fulfillment") is showing the visitor around the sect's large and busy premises in a western suburb of Tōkyō. He wears a black robe and carries a rosary, but carefully states that he is a layman, that their sect, founded in 1938, is entirely a lay movement. They take the *Lotus Sūtra* (see p. 64) as their chief scripture, and find in it not only the essence of Mahāyāna Buddhism but a guide to life in a modern industrial society. As he talks, flocks of pretty young women in traditional costume sail by. The official says that his sect does not believe in coercive proselytizing and political activism, like its rival Sōka Gakkai, nor does it practice faith healing like some other new sects. It concentrates instead on solving life problems through application of Buddhist principles. He shows a large hall where numerous groups, each of about ten people, are engaging in discussion under guidance of a leader. The guide says that modern Japanese cities are filled with uprooted people who need friends and substitutes for traditional families and village communities.

They come to the sect's chief chapel, an enormous round building with a many-galleried interior like a European opera house. It can hold ten thousand people, the guide says. The visitor reminds himself that not all mass movements that hold gigantic rallies and revere charismatic leaders can justly be accused of fascist tendencies.

The United States

Three hundred members of the Young Buddhist Association are attending the annual seminar in a seaside park near Monterrey. Of the forty in the advanced discussion section, thirty are Japanese Americans, the rest European Americans. The point in dispute is whether American Buddhists should be socially active, should support integration, work for racial equality, and give aid to the Buddhists of Vietnam. The young minister, a recent immigrant from Japan, diffidently but staunchly presents the orthodox viewpoint of old-country Jōdo Shinshū that, though Buddhists as individuals may participate in sociopolitical action, Buddhist institutions should neither participate in nor endorse such action. An American graduate student points out that in the sixteenth century this same sect led a mass revolt of peasants against their feudal lords and became a feudal power in its own right. Under pressure from the Americans, the minister finally admits that his own sympathies are with them rather than with the orthodox view of his sect.

England

The three-story house is distinguished from others on the London street only by its yellow front door. Upstairs, an English Buddhist monk, home after fifteen years in India, sits on a Tibetan carpet under a Tibetan scroll-painting. Every five minutes the phone rings, and the monk deals in a brisk office voice with another piece of business. The Sangha Association committee handles finances and administration, but the lecture program, meeting inquirers, and public relations leave him little time for study and meditation. The monk speaks enthusiastically about a meditation center his group is starting in an old mansion in the countryside. Beside him sit two novices who are preparing to go to India for full ordination and training.

India Again

Three Westerners—a musician turned contemplative, a Zionist in search of a meditation master, and an orientalist—sit talking in a hill town. All three are willing to call themselves Buddhists but are ill at ease when non-Buddhists do so. The musician has been practicing meditation daily for several months. His face has the special mobile radiance of the contemplative. He speaks spontaneously to the occasion, with implicit authenticity. The Zionist chronicles his career from law-school dropout ("They kept giving me fellowships but I realized it would ruin my mind") to kibbutznik ("It's a wonderful way of life, but when you've got it, what are you going to do with it?") to itinerant seeker. The orientalist quietly cherishes his newly consolidated realization that he has finally reconciled his scholarship and his religion.

They speak of the general dissolution of old institutions and doctrines, of chaos as the beginning of new creation, of an imminent resurgence of intuitive wisdom, and of enlightenment as the cardinal source of justice. They sense a turning point in history when, after enduring for millenia, conventional wisdom crumbles and new world views stand revealed.

2.
Life and Teachings of Gautama the Buddha

The Historical Setting

The sixth century B.C. was one of the most pivotal in the history of India. It marked the shift from tribal oligarchies to monarchies and empires, the growth and multiplication of cities, the quickening of trade, increasing craft specialization, beginnings of a monetary sector in the economy, development of bureaucratic institutions, and emergence of two new classes, the rich merchants and the professional royal advisers. During this century there arose a welter of nonsacerdotal religious teachings which pushed the Vedic orthodoxy from dominance in the middle Ganges area, the very region where social change was most advanced. Incomparably the most successful of these sects was Buddhism, essentially because it combined appropriateness to its original time and place with the capacity to spread and adapt itself to other situations.

The Upaniṣads

By the early sixth century B.C., Brāhmanical thinkers in the Upaniṣads were deprecating ritual action and extolling the power of thought. They affirmed the older mythic idea that the Primordial Being created the world by thinking (or willing). Mind for these archaic Indians was objective, a subtle substance that is all-pervasive, that goes everywhere on its own ethereal plane. It is thus a sort of god, just as the senses are termed gods in the Upaniṣads because they are sentient, unseen powers. If this is the case, it seems reasonable that by taking thought one can not only increase one's stature (compare Matthew 6:27) but transform one's entire state of being.

The early Upaniṣads identified the self (*ātman*) of the person with the indwelling world power (*brahman*). He who knows the meaning of something, they thought, has grasped its essence and controls it. So he who knows the identity of his own essence and the cosmic power becomes divine and "is magnified in the world of Brahmā." An outstanding feature of the Brahmā-world is that beings there do not die and go to rebirth elsewhere.

Belief in transmigration was not Vedic, but came into prominence about 600 B.C., at first as an attempt to explain the cycles of life in the natural world.

The spirits of the dead go either on the path of the gods (*deva*) to the solar world of Brahmā, or on the path of the "fathers" to the moon, where they are eaten by the gods and descend again to become rain which is absorbed by plants, which are eaten by men and animals and converted into semen, which engenders further animal life. The lunar path involves repeated dying, and so is undesirable because death is painful, not because life is miserable. So the goal of early Upaniṣadic striving is to reach the world of Brahmā, from which people do not return. Early texts are vague as to whether the Brahmā-world is a paradise or a formless, inconceivable state, whether it is the top zone of space or a nonspatial realm. They agree that deserving souls go there after death, and that the decisive factors are one's deeds during life and the purpose that rules the mind at the moment of death. The practice that leads to the immortal realm is devout meditation (*upāsanā*) upon the immortal part of oneself, and the main philosophical problem is to identify this part and distinguish it from the other, perishable parts.

The Ascetic Movement

The Vedic priesthood and the Upaniṣadic sages were householders, observing celibacy only during the student years, and affirming the value of the procreative act. In the sixth century, the celibate ascetic (*śramaṇa*) appeared on the scene. These "strivers" abandoned family life, generally gave up normal work and lived by begging, and wandered around from village to village, dwelling in the forest and forming unstable congregations around masters who propounded a wild diversity of teachings. Some materialists taught that there is no afterlife, that when the four elements (earth, water, fire, and air) separate at death, the senses and mind dissolve into space. Some held that the highest happiness is to enjoy the pleasures of this world. Most, though, believed in transmigration, and maintained that life is misery and that liberation from the cycle of birth and death is the supreme good. The materialists thought that the soul and the body are identical, while the others thought that soul and body are different. In general, though, the śramaṇas placed more emphasis on ascetic regimen than on knowledge as a means to liberation.

The old tales in the *Mahābhārata* describe austerities (*tapas*) undertaken to win the favor of deities, who when duly propitiated appear to the devotee and grant his boon—give him offspring, or answer his question. The śramaṇas, though, were not worshippers of the deities, but accumulators of merit, a spiritual currency as impersonal and public as gold. The post-Vedic brāhmans had reduced sacrifice to a mechanical determinism such that the gods had no option but to comply. Since it was human action that made the rites efficacious, the gods became redundant, and the śramaṇas dispensed with them. The sacrificing priests were crass mercenaries who collected fees and earned no merit, since merit is the spiritual compensation for material rewards foregone.

The śramaṇas lived in poverty and strove for imperishable and inalienable riches. Among the chief fruits of their exertions were magic and spiritual powers.

The ascetics who believe in an individual soul distinct from the body consider austerity a means of purification. First the body is purged of dark, coarse, bad matter. Then the soul is cleansed of material stains and finally liberated from transmigrant bodies. This is the position of Jainism, whose great master Mahāvīra was a contemporary of the Buddha. The Jains hold that action (*karman*) is a special kind of subtle matter which darkens and binds the naturally bright and free soul. Bad deeds are more adhesive and pollute the soul more than good deeds, which are easily dispelled. So the ascetic must overcome bad action with good action, and then overcome good action through inaction. Austerity eliminates karman already incurred, and restraint prevents the influx of new karman. The "victors" (*jina*) or "adepts" (*arhant*) achieve liberation while in the body, but live out their last life through the force of residual karman. Mahāvīra, thirty years after becoming a jina, achieved final release from the body by fasting to death.

The Jains say that the pure soul is omniscient and perfectly blissful. Matter, then, is the obstacle to exercise of the paranormal powers. It veils perception and impedes motion. So, of course, austerity frees the innate magic faculties of the holy man.

Tapas ("austerity, heat") was associated in archaic Indian thought with procreation, cosmic and animal. "That One was born through the power of heat [*tapas*]. In the beginning there arose desire [*kāma*], which was the first semen of mind/will [*manas*]" (*Rig Veda* 10.129, 3–4). It was believed that emission of semen depleted one's vital force, so the aspirant to paranormal attainments ought to conserve his energy by practicing continence. Moderation, though commended to the householder, would not suffice for the ascetic, who strove for perfection. Moreover, celibacy was convenient, since a man without family could live and travel as he pleased, and a reputation for chastity assured the wandering stranger of a better welcome from householders.

Why did men want to become wizards and adepts? Only some were strongly impelled to achieve release from transmigration. The majority were professionals, happy to become "worthy of reverence, worthy of offerings." Householders gained merit by donation to a holy man, by feeding and ministering to him. Hospitality was a cardinal virtue among the Indo-Aryans. Any guest was to be treated as a god, and a holy man especially so. In return, adepts used their supernormal insight to solve the problems of petitioners. They gave diagnoses and made predictions, advised on policy and warned of dangers. To this day, Buddhist monks and Hindu renunciants continue to practice these useful arts.

The quest for the ultimate lured an adventurous minority who were not content with merely deserving the alms they received. Conversely, the ordinary ascetic enjoyed greater prestige if his path had led famous saints to perfection.

Competition and consequently transcendence were built right into the ascetic movement.

Gautama the Buddha: History and Myth

The extant versions of the complete life of the Buddha were all composed five hundred or more years after his death. They draw on much earlier material from the canonical *Sūtras* ("Discourses") and *Vinaya* ('Discipline") for events after the Renunciation. Except for sporadic incidents, they tell a legendary account of his earlier life, a fabric of myth and literary invention. The authors viewed the Buddha as an epic hero, and their purpose was to celebrate his deeds; they were not chroniclers but poets. Nonetheless, Aśvaghoṣa (first century A.D.), in his *Acts of the Buddha,* saw Gautama as a genuine human being; and even where the narrative is not historical, it is dramatically authentic. The hero is a man experiencing conflicts, undergoing genuine temptations, trying and ultimately rejecting false courses, at every point exercising choice and prevailing, not through fate or the intervention of other men or gods, but through his own action. He is motivated by compassion for suffering mankind, and he exhibits the martial virtues of courage, steadfastness, initiative, and self-discipline. He sustains a delicate sensitivity and an unshakable dignity.

How close is this attractive character to the historical person? Probably as close as Aśvaghoṣa could make it with the data and concepts at his disposal. The quest for the objective Gautama, like that for the historical Jesus, is foredoomed to a measure of failure. We cannot get behind the portrait that the early communities synthesized for their founders; their reports are all we have. But though the Community (*Saṅgha*) created the image of the Buddha, the Buddha created the Community and in so doing impressed upon it his personality. The master exhorted his disciples to imitate him, and they formulated and transmitted an image of him, along with his teachings, as a model for later generations to imitate. Though the process of formulation entails distortion, the purpose of transmission assures a measure of fidelity.

Birth and Youth of the Bodhisattva

The Śākyas were a *kṣatriya* ("warrior") tribe inhabiting a border district just below the Himālayan foothills. For some unknown reason, they used the brāhman clan name Gautama ("descendent of the sage Gotama"). The future Buddha's father, Śuddhodana, was a prince of Kapilavastu, a town for which archeologists have not been able to find remains.

Śākyamuni ("Sage of the Śākyas") was born in about 560 B.C.[1] Buddhists

[1] The chronology of Gautama's life hinges on the date of his death, which in turn is variously assigned by the regional Buddhist traditions. Modern scholars, calculating back from the dates of the emperor Aśoka, have agreed within a few years: Thomas, 563–483 B.C.; Filliozat, 559–478 (*Inde Classique,* nos. 375, 376, pp. 2178, 2209).

celebrate his nativity on the full moon of Vaiśākha (April–May), the fourth month in the Indian calendar. The legend says that he was immaculately conceived when his mother, Māyā, dreamed that a white elephant entered her body. When her time was approaching, she retired to the wooded garden of Lumbinī, near Kapilavastu, where, standing with her upstretched right hand on the branch of a tree, she gave birth to the bodhisattva ("future Buddha"). The newborn child stood up, strode seven paces, and declared that this was his last birth, that he was destined for enlightenment. Asita, an aged rishi, came, examined the marks on the infant, and prophesied that he would become a Buddha. They called the boy Siddhārtha, "He who has achieved his goal."

The purpose of all the mythic elements in the nativity cycle is to show that the bodhisattva was innately different from ordinary men. The view that normal procreation and birth are impure betrays a body image in sharp contrast to the Upaniṣads, which liken copulation to sacrifice.

Seven days after giving birth, Māyā died. Śuddhodana married her sister Prajāpatī, who brought up the young bodhisattva. When he came of age, he was married to a bride, usually called Yaśodharā, whom his father selected. The legend embellishes this phase with epic and folklore motifs, saying that Śuddhodana tried to prevent his son from becoming an ascetic by tying him down with sensual pleasures, not only arranging his marriage but surrounding him with song-and-dance girls.

In due course Yaśodharā bore Siddhārtha a son, whom they named Rāhula, "The Fetter," an indication that the young father's heart was already turning away from the household life.

The Great Renunciation

The legend tells that Prince Siddhārtha, secluded by his overprotective father from every hint of sorrow and suffering, went out for a chariot ride and for the first time saw a decrepit old man. Shocked, he asked his charioteer about the man's condition; the charioteer declared that such is the destiny of all men. The prince turned back to the palace and brooded in melancholy, taking no relish in the gaity and pleasure around him. On a second ride, he saw his first diseased man, and reflected that people are foolish to remain gay under the constant threat of disease. On the third trip, he saw his first corpse, was stricken with dismay, and marveled that men could forget the fear of death and live heedlessly.

The brooding prince rode out again, observed the peasants plowing, and, unlike the ordinary patrician, was moved to grief at the suffering of men and oxen, and even at the slaughter of worms and insects by the plow. He sat under a tree, entered the first trance, and found some peace of mind. He meditated on the truth of suffering. After a while he saw a religious mendicant, and made up his mind to leave the household life.

The legend poignantly describes how in the depth of night the prince took a last look at his wife and infant son, mounted his horse, and rode out of the sleeping city, accompanied by his charioteer. Siddhārtha dismounted, sent his charioteer back to Śuddhodana with his ornaments and a message, then cut off his hair and exchanged clothes with a passing hunter.

The kernel of this episode, the Great Renunciation, is the conflict between the household and the ascetic ways of life. Far from encouraging his son to become a monk, Śuddhodana did everything in his power to prevent him. And at each point, Siddhārtha recognized his duty and expressed strong affection toward his father. Aśvaghoṣa puts into the bodhisattva's mouth a speech justifying departure for the homeless life as fidelity to an even higher *Dharma* ("duty, norm").

The Bodhisattva's Studies

The new mendicant, then twenty-nine years old, went first to a teacher called Ārāḍa Kālāma, who apparently taught a kind of meditation leading to "attainment of the state of nothing at all." His means were faith, energy, mindfulness, concentration, and wisdom. Gautama practiced the method and quickly attained the goal. Kālāma then set him up as his equal and coteacher. But Gautama concluded that this doctrine (Dharma) did not lead to enlightenment and nirvāṇa and went away. He then studied under Udraka Rāmaputra, who taught the way to the "attainment of neither conception nor nonconception." Gautama mastered this dharma, was acclaimed a teacher, found it unsatisfactory, and abandoned it.

The canonical account of Gautama's study under these two teachers is an old one, formulated in the concepts and literary modes of the early Buddhist church, but otherwise plausible. What the teachers and their illustrious disciple were pursuing was not contemplative identification of the soul and the world spirit (like the Upaniṣads), not starving out impurities through abstinence (like the Jains), but attainment of enlightenment (*bodhi*) and *nirvāṇa* (etymologically, "blowing out, expiration") through cultivation of trances.

The account indicates the attainments of the two teachers with reference to another early Buddhist formula, the eight liberations (*vimokṣa*). The meditator, passing beyond perceptions of visible form (*rūpa*), ceases to perceive diversity and abides in stage four, awareness of the infinity of consciousness, then awareness of nothing at all, then awareness of neither conception nor nonconception, then finally the cessation of conception and feeling. Ārāḍa's attainment is stage six, and Uddaka's is stage seven. The author of the canonical account may have taken this means to express a hazy tradition that the Buddha's teachers had almost but not quite realized the highest trance attainment, or, on the other hand, the formula may have originated in the Buddha's systematization of his own experience.

The technique indicated is to contemplate things that have shape-cum-color (*rūpa*) until they become transparent. Solid objects and their corresponding sensory images dissolve; the meditator escapes from the confines of his solid body and in ecstasy abides in his mind-body. The four form-plane elements (earth, water, fire, and air) are transcended. Then as the consciousness of the yogin becomes subtler and more all-pervasive, he transcends awareness of the fifth element, space-ether (*ākāśa*) and then of the sixth element, consciousness. In this stage, the awareness of nothing at all, there is still consciousness but it is so subtle that no object corresponds to it. But conceptions and feelings evidently remain. The seventh stage is the terminus of the formless plane, at the end point of existence, so it is fittingly expressed in the pattern "neither *X* nor non-*X*" which commonly indicates in Buddhist language a point at which the series is transcended and opposites merge.

Gautama forsook the dharma of the two teachers because it did not conduce to "aversion, dispassion, cessation, tranquility, superknowledge, enlightenment, and nirvāṇa," says the Sūtra. These seven quasi-synonyms taken together show the main features of the goal that Gautama sought: pacification of mental turbulence, perfect direct knowledge, and attainment of the unconditioned realm.

His Austerities

The bodhisattva then went eastward to Uruvelā near Gayā, where he found a pleasant spot and settled down to austerities. He practiced stopping his breath to induce trances, and was not deterred by the violent headaches that resulted. He fasted and came as close as he could to eating nothing at all, with the result that he became utterly emaciated. He was joined in his strivings by five ascetics, and continued in this painful course until six years after the Great Renunciation. Then he realized that by this severe mortification he had not achieved sublime knowledge and insight, and he tried to think of another way. He remembered the incident in his childhood when he sat under a shady tree while his father was plowing. His mind had happened on a dispassionate equilibrium and he had entered the first trance (dhyāna), a pleasant and zestful state. Perhaps this pointed to a fruitful method. But his body was too weak and lean, he realized, to gain this blissful exaltation.

The legend says that Gautama then sat under another sacred tree. A woman named Sujātā had vowed a yearly offering to this tree if she obtained a son. The wish was fulfilled, and she prepared as offering a fine bowl of rice milk. Her maid came upon the bodhisattva sitting there, mistook him for the spirit of the tree, and reported the apparition to her mistress, who came and presented the food to Gautama. The Pali Sūtra says simply that Gautama took solid food, rice, and yogurt. The five mendicants then left him in disgust, saying that he had given up striving and was living in abundance.

Gautama's rejection of extreme austerities hinged on a critical moment when he realized that in his childhood he had known a state of happiness free from sensual desires and immoral thoughts. It dawned on him that there was nothing wrong with being happy. He went on to recognize that a healthy body is necessary for the pursuit of wisdom. In so doing, he turned toward enlightenment and took the first step on the Middle Way which became the central point of his Dharma. While rejecting both mortification of the flesh and sensual indulgence, he accepted happiness as good. Moreover, when he broke his fast he affirmed in the act that the person is not a soul-substance alien to the body, but an organic entity in which both physical and psychic factors participate.

Temptation by Māra

According to the legend, Gautama on the fourteenth of Vaiśākha dreamed five dreams indicating that he was about to become a Buddha. The next day, he accepted the meal from Sujātā. He went and sat under the Bodhi Tree, facing east, and resolved not to arise until he attained enlightenment. Māra the Evil One was alarmed at the prospect of the Bodhisattva's victory, and came to assail him with an army of fearful demons. The Bodhisattva was protected, though, by his accumulated merit and his friendly love (*maitrī*). After failing to shake him, the hosts of demons fled in defeat. Māra then invoked his own merit so as to convert it into magic power and overthrow the Bodhisattva. But Gautama invoked his own superior merit, amassed through many previous lives. Māra called on his retinue to witness his merit; and Śākyamuni, having no other witness on his side, touched the earth with his right hand (a pose often shown in Buddhist art), and called Mother Earth to testify to his merit. The earth quaked in response. Then Māra, having failed with intimidation and compulsion, turned to temptation. He sent his three daughters, Discontent, Delight, and Desire, to seduce the future Buddha, who remained as impervious to lust as he had to fear. As the sun set, Māra and his hosts gave up and withdrew.

This temptation episode is quite a late addition and entirely mythical. The myth, though, is a suitable expression of an experience common to most contemplatives. The seeker eventually commits himself to an integral attempt, overcomes doubt and inertia, and sets to work. This conjures up the demons of fear from the unconscious. All the habit-hardened dispositions protest against their coming destruction. But good habits sustain the seeker's resolve. The waves of fear pass, and doubts arise as to whether the candidate is really equal to the challenge. If he possesses genuine self-confidence, the doubts are vanquished. The last peril is of course the rosiest and the deadliest. Perfect love (*maitrī*) may cast out fear, but it all too easily changes into libido.

The Enlightenment

On the night of the full moon, the Bodhisattva ascended the four stages of trance (*dhyāna*). The first trance is produced by detaching from sense objects and calming the passions. It is marked by zest and ease, and thinking in it is discursive, focusing and gazing at the mental images as they pass. Similar trances sometimes occur spontaneously when the mind is concentrated, stimulated, and focused steadily on one object by love or hate, intellectual discovery or artistic inspiration. The second trance is nondiscursive. There is one-pointedness of mind, serene faith, zest, and ease. The third trance is dispassionate rather than zestful; it is mindful and conscious, with a feeling of bliss in the body. The fourth trance is free from opposites such as pleasure and pain, elation and depression. It is pure awareness and equanimity.

All of the trances are characterized by concentration and accurate cognition. The insight they facilitate is not theoretical knowledge but direct perception. They lead to the six "superknowledges": (1) magic powers (such as levitation and walking on water), (2) the divine ear, (3) knowledge of others' minds, (4) memory of one's former lives, (5) the divine eye, (6) and extinction of the "outflows," namely sensual desire, desire for coming to be, and ignorance. The first five are mundane, while the sixth is realized only by the perfected saint (*arhant*). It distinguishes the liberated adept from the mere wizard.

During the first watch of the night (evening), Gautama acquired the first cognition, that of his own previous existences one by one, seeing them just as they had been.

During the second watch (midnight) he acquired the divine eye (the fifth superknowledge and second cognition), with which he surveyed the decease and rebirth of living beings everywhere. The whole universe, it is said, appeared to him as in a mirror. He saw that good deeds lead to a happy rebirth and evil deeds to a miserable next life.

During the third watch (late night), he acquired the third cognition (and sixth superknowledge), that of the extinction of the outflows. He perceived the Four Holy Truths, noting, "This is suffering, this is the source of suffering, this is the cessation of suffering, and this is the path that leads to the cessation of suffering." According to Aśvaghoṣa, he realized the principle of "dependent arising," and meditated on the twelve "preconditions." His mind became free from the outflows, and as the Sūtra says, "In me emancipated arose knowledge of my emancipation. I realized that rebirth has been destroyed, the holy life has been lived, the job has been done, there is nothing after this."

The new day dawned on Gautama, now the Buddha. According to legend the animate and natural worlds celebrated the event with prodigies. The earth swayed, thunder rolled and rain fell from a cloudless sky, blossoms fell from the heavens, and Gautama's ancestors, then sages in paradise, observed his victory and offered him reverence. The Buddha thus acquited on a higher level the family obligation that, as a Bodhisattva, he had forsaken in the worldly sense.

Interpretation of the Enlightenment

What actually happened on the night of the Enlightenment? The oldest account is stylized and exhibits typical mythic features. It purports, though, to be autobiographical, and the claim may be substantially true. First-person reporting of "peak experiences" was not a genre in pre-Buddhist Indian literature, and flourished only sporadically in later centuries. Implicit in it is the affirmation that the particular experiences of a historical person are of outstanding value. The dignity, economy, and sobriety of the account not only highlight the magnitude of Gautama's claims, but strongly suggest a remarkable man behind the style, self-assured and self-aware, assertive but not bombastic. If disciples put such words into the mouth of their master, then who put into their minds such an image of him?

Later doctrine elaborates the idea of "the silence of the saints" and holds that nirvāṇa is indescribable; but nowhere does the early Canon say that the content of the Enlightenment is nonintellectual, or that it is inexpressible. However splendid the visions and however exalted the mystic state of mind, the Enlightenment consisted of the discovery of communicable ideas. It is described as the realization in trance of the specific destinies of all living beings and of the general principles governing these destinies. The first cognition, memory of one's own former lives, is a shamanic power, documented even among the Amerindians. The second cognition, perception of living beings everywhere dying and being reborn, is likewise a variety of shamanic power—unobstructed cosmic vision—widely attested in archaic cultures. It evidently involves seeing the past and future, as well as the present, condition of others, a power universally attributed to prophets. The specifically Buddhist feature is correlating good deeds with happy births and bad deeds with miserable ones. The third cognition is a philosophical theory (Greek *theōria,* "a seeing, a vision, a contemplation"). It is presented not as the fruits of speculation but as a direct perception, like the first two cognitions. The phrasing looks rather abstract to the modern reader, but clearly it was intended, for all its generality, to be experiential and concrete. The universals that Gautama saw were simply the aggregates of observable particulars. The content of enlightenment is thus two-thirds shamanism ethically transformed, and one-third philosophy, a feature that higher civilization does not share with the archaic and the primitive.

The sequence of nocturnal watches matched with the three cognitions, and the coincidence of daybreak and enlightenment, are mythic but not necessarily fictitious. Many a man has sat rapt in thought all night and has seen his solution in a flood of light as his whole being quickened to the new day. The initiant into Mediterranean mystery cults sat in darkness until he saw a great light. Darkness is an objective aid to sensory withdrawal, without which the inner light cannot burst into radiance. The Eskimo aspirant to shamanhood passes long hours in solitary meditation, and in the climactic moment feels a mysterious light in his body, especially in his brain, which enables him to see in the dark as well as to see the future and other occult things. The light in question, with shaman and bhikṣu, is not just a figure of speech, but a physical experience of overwhelming radiance. The experience is described often and vividly in meditation manuals. It has obvious analogies with certain experiences under psychedelic drugs, and may perhaps have a similar physiological basis. In any event greatly heightened sensitivity is a factor.

The full moon may be a ritual element in the story. The nights when the moon changes phase were considered ominous in ancient India, and celebrated with fasts and rites, especially the new and full moons. Other Wanderer sects were celebrating these dates by assembling and preaching their doctrine, so at the instance of his followers the Buddha prescribed that his Community should do likewise. The ritual high point of the month, the night of the full moon, would have seemed most appropriate for the Enlightenment, and the event may in fact have taken place then. One can imagine the effect on Gautama's psyche of the cool moonlit tropical night scene.

As already remarked, the Enlightenment fused archaic shamanic attainments with an ethical and philosophical vision. The primitive elements are in service to the higher ones. The first and second cognitions constitute an empirical verification of the doctrines of transmigration and retribution for deeds. In Gautama's view, the materialists who say that there is no afterlife and that there is no fruition of past deeds are as wrong as the dualists who hold that there is a soul separate from the body. What determines one's rebirth, though, is not sacrifice or mere gnosis, as in the Upaniṣads, but the quality of one's entire life. Those who do good in deed, word, and thought, who speak well of the saints and hold right views, are reborn in a happy state, in paradise. Those who do evil are reborn in a wretched state, in hell.

The idea of moral causality seems only in the sixth century B.C. to have become dissociated from notions of the efficacy of ritual and ascetic acts. There is no assurance that Upaniṣadic passages expressing the idea are pre-Buddhist. If, as is probable, Gautama discovered this comprehensive moral world view, it is no wonder that the vision burst upon him with revelatory force, that he saw the principle enacted in a cosmic panorama of doing, dying, and rebirth.

One novel feature of early Buddhist ethics is that it gives primacy to intention. Good and bad are not quasi-physical as in Jainism, but are assigned to a distinct moral dimension. Unintentional deeds have merely commonsense consequences, not karmic ones. The *Vinaya* ("Discipline") regularly distinguishes deliberate from inadvertent violations of the rule. In contrast to later Hinduism, the physical act is of itself neither pure nor impure. Gautama's achievement in freeing ethics from ritual and tabu was as momentous as Paul's emancipation of Christianity from the Jewish Torah.

The Twelve Preconditions

The variant accounts of what Gautama realized during the third watch agree that he found the cause and the cure for transmigration. They differ in doctrinal formulation, which is perhaps a secondary matter, since the twin causes are invariably desire and ignorance, and the cure is knowledge. As he proclaimed the Four Holy Truths in his first sermon a few weeks later, he may well have "seen" them (in the manner of a Vedic seer "seeing" a hymn) during the night of the Enlightenment.

The formula of the twelve "preconditions" is an ancient one, and accords well with the context of the third watch, since it is a general statement of patterns relating to the pageant of transmigration observed in the second watch. The Pali Vinaya says that after the Enlightenment the Buddha sat in meditation at the foot of the Bodhi Tree for seven days, and that on the seventh night he contemplated the twelve preconditions, running through the chain forward and backward once in each of the three watches of the night. Thus even though the formula is not mentioned in the Pali Sūtra account, the early Buddhist tradition associated it with the Enlightenment.

The twelve preconditions are: (1) ignorance, (2) dispositions, (3) consciousness, (4) name-and-form, (5) the six sense fields, (6) contact, (7) feeling, (8) craving, (9) appropriation, (10) becoming, (11) birth, and (12) aging and dying.

Causation, a central problem throughout the history of Indian philosophy, first drew consideration in early archaic speculation about creation. The question was, simply and vaguely, how the world came into existence. Gautama's question, though, was not how the manifested world came to be projected or created from the unmanifest, but what suffering depends on and how it can be stopped. He began at the end of the chain and worked backward, observing that:

(12) aging and dying depend on birth (if there were no birth, then there would be no death);

(11) birth depends on becoming (if life *X* did not die and come to be life *Y*, there would be no birth of *Y*);

(10) becoming depends on appropriation (if the life process did not appropriate phenomenal materials just as a fire appropriates fuel, then there would be no transmigration);

(9) appropriation depends on craving (if one did not thirst for sense objects, for coming to be after this life, and for ceasing to be after this life, then the transmigrant process would not appropriate fuel);

(8) craving depends on feeling (if pleasant and painful feelings were not experienced, then one would not be conditioned to seek continuing experience of the pleasant or cessation of the unpleasant);

(7) feeling depends on contact (the meeting of sense and object is necessary before pleasure or pain can be felt);

(6) contact depends on the six sense fields (the six pairs of sense and datum, namely eye–rūpa, ear–sound, smelling–smell, tongue–taste, body–touchable, mind–dharma);

(5) the six sense fields depend on name-and-form (mind and body; as the sense fields are equivalent to name-and-form, some lists of the preconditions omit the sense fields);

(4) name-and-form, the whole living organism, depends on consciousness,

which here means the spark of sentient life that enters the womb and animates the embryo;

(3) consciousness depends on the dispositions accrued throughout life as karmic residues of deeds, words, and thoughts;

(2) and the karmic legacy that produces rebirth depends on ignorance of the Four Holy Truths;

(1) ignorance.

Gautama's prescription is: When ignorance ceases, dispositions cease, and so on until aging and dying cease.

Each precondition depends on the one before it, and evidently ignorance is held to depend on aging and dying, so that the twelve preconditions form a circle, represented in Buddhist art as the Wheel of Life. The logical character of the chain is shown by the affirmative and negative forms: "If *B* exists, then *A* has existed. If *A* does not exist, then *B* will not exist." The relation between the links is implication. As a theory of causation, this "dependent arising" concerns the formal concomitances between things rather than their material derivation from one another. It resembles a medical diagnosis in several ways. By showing that the ailment depends on a series of conditions, it indicates the point at which the series can be broken and so facilitates a cure. This counteracts the theory that the disease is a fortuitous happening, against which no remedy would be effective, and also opposes the view that the ultimate cause of the malady is some entity outside the process, such as God or an immutable soul. Salvation from transmigration is to be found in the process of transmigration itself.

The Decision to Propagate Dharma

Tradition says that the Buddha spent forty-nine days in the neighborhood of the Bodhi Tree. Then two merchants en route from Orissa passed close by, and were advised by the spirit of a dead relative that they should go and make offerings to the new Buddha who was sitting at the foot of a certain tree. They offered honey cakes and sugar cane and "took refuge" in the Buddha and his Dharma, thus becoming the first Buddhists and the first lay devotees in the world.

Note that Gautama did not preach Dharma to the two men, but merely received their reverence and offerings. Worship of holy men is nonsectarian and does not involve subscribing to the man's ideas. Buddhist lay cult is here shown developing naturally out of pre-Buddhist practices. We shall later see more examples of the spirits informing, advising, and inspiring men. Observe again that the ties of human kinship hold even after rebirth in the spirit species.

The canonical account says that the Buddha then thought that mankind, addicted to its attachments, would find it hard to understand his Dharma. If he tried and they did not understand, this would weary and vex him. Brahmā, the highest god in the popular religion of the time, read the Buddha's mind, left the Brahmā-world, appeared in front of the Buddha, and pleaded, "May the Blessed One teach the Dharma, May the Well-gone One teach the Dharma. There are living beings with little dust in their eyes who fall away through not hearing the Dharma. They will be recognizers of the Dharma." Then, out of compassion for living beings, Śākyamuni surveyed the world with his Buddha-eye and saw that some beings had little impurity and some had much, that some had keen faculties and some had dull ones. Realizing that there was a suitable audience, he decided to proclaim the Dharma.

Either Gautama actually experienced an apparition, or this tale is a fiction. In either case, it expresses a critical choice that he must have made. If he had not decided to return and act in the world, his withdrawal would have been insignificant for human history. The stated motive for his reconsideration was compassion. This virtue, the peer of wisdom and superior to all others, figures prominently in Mahāyāna Buddhology, but also is regularly ascribed to the Buddha in the Pali Canon. The Buddha, furthermore, observes the Āryan gentleman's etiquette; he does not thrust his doctrine on those who are unready to accept it, and he waits for an invitation. Since he was to be the teacher of gods and men, who else but Great Brahmā was worthy to invite him?

The Hierarchy of Beings

Early Buddhist texts frequently mention various species of spirits, but do not consider them especially sacred. The Buddhas and *arhants* ("perfected saints") are superior to even the highest gods who, like lower beings, are still subject to karmic retribution. Men should treat spirits like human guests or holy men, and make food offerings to them. Malignant spirits should not be appeased with sacrifice but should be tamed through the power of a holy man.

The world consists of three realms, one above the other: the desire realm, the form realm, and the formless realm. Within these realms are located various "destinies," classes of animate beings.

The lowest beings are the inhabitants of the hells, which are hot and cold subterranean places of agelong but not everlasting retribution. Next lowest are the *pretas* ("ghosts") who haunt the earth's surface. They are continually tormented by hunger, and stand outside walls and gates, mutely pleading to be fed.

Animals rank just above the pretas, though the category is somewhat confused by inclusion of the nāgas and other mythical beasts and birds. The *nāgas* are water spirits, inhabiting rivers, lakes, and oceans. They are either dragons or cobras, an ambivalence which indicates that the cult is hybrid. Like men, they can be either protective or destructive. The enemies of the *nāgas* are the *garuḍas,* half man and half bird of prey.

The human destiny is the lowest and most important of the fortunate ones, for only in it can virtue and wisdom be increased. Even when someone attains nirvāṇa while sojourning in a heaven, it is the result of the ripening of merit he won as a human being. Man stands in the middle of the animate hierarchy, not, as in the post-Darwinian world view, at the top.

A motley crowd of spirits inhabits the earth's surface and the lower atmosphere. The *asuras* ("titans"), ancient rivals of the gods (*deva*), are fierce giants, sometimes but not always wicked, intensely proud, and jealous. But they are shown as keeping the precepts, practicing donation, and worshipping the Buddha. The *yakṣas* are primarily tree spirits, especially present in the sap, the living water, and producing fertility and growth. They were the chief divinities of the popular non-Vedic cult, were intimately associated with early Buddhism, and supplied features to the pantheons and cults of classical Hinduism and Mahāyāna Buddhism.

The most illustrious *yakṣas* are the Four Great Kings, also called world-protectors, each of whom rules one of the cardinal points. Kubera, also called Vaiśravaṇa, ruler of the North, was widely worshipped as the god of wealth.

The *gandharvas* in the *Rig Veda* were spirits of the clouds and waters, and so were associated with fertility. In their aerial aspect, as cloud spirits, the gandharvas came to be musicians attendant upon the gods. As divinities of streams and ponds, the gandharvas rival the nāgas, with whom they are said to have once waged war and lost. Gandharvas mate with *apsarases* ("nymphs"), and such couples, in human form, are frequently shown in art.

Goddesses are seldom mentioned in early Buddhist texts. The goddess of fortune, Śrī or Lakṣmī, is named in the Pali Canon, and appears in Buddhist art of the second century B.C., standing, or sitting on her lotus pediment and being bathed by two elephants.

The second rank of celestials in the desire realm are the Gods of the Thirty-Three, the old pantheon of the Rig Veda headed by Indra, more generally called Śakra in Buddhist texts. He is devout, reveres the Buddha and protects the Dharma. Buddhist propagandists evidently presented the reformed character of the soma-quaffing barbarian god of the Rig Veda as a model for their kṣatriya converts. Śakra figures prominently in Pali texts, even more so in Mahāyāna Sūtras. Buddhist texts do not urge worship of him, but his protection is heartily appreciated.

The Buddhists superimposed on the old Vedic Thirty-Three four more tiers of desire-realm gods, of which only the second, *Tuṣita* ("Satisfied"), is important. The bodhisattva spends his last life there before he becomes a Buddha.

Four classes of gods are assigned to the form realm, but the pantheon in fact stops with the first, the Gods of Brahmā's retinue. No gods are named as rulers of the higher planes, and the Brahmā-world is repeatedly cited as the upper limit of "this world."

In the Buddhist myths Brahmā claims to see everything, so it is appropriate that he should tell the hesitant Buddha that there are living beings who are ready to recognize the Dharma. Then and only then did the Buddha use his Buddha-eye to confirm this fact. The Canon commonly presents inspiration as a message from a god. It seems unnecessary for a spirit to inform an adept of something that he could have known through his super-knowledge, but then ordinary people often have to be told things they could have seen for themselves if they had just looked.

The First Sermon

Having decided to proclaim his doctrine, Gautama, moved by filial piety, thought first of telling his two former teachers; but a deity informed him that Ārāḍa had died a week before, and that Udraka had died the previous night. The Buddha confirmed this with his superknowledge, then thought of the five mendicants who had shared his austerities. With his divine eye he saw that they were staying near Benares, so he set out.

On the road, Gautama met an ascetic who remarked on his clear eyes and radiant complexion and asked about his religion. The Buddha declared that he was a Victor, that he had no equal in the world of gods and men, that he had become omniscient and had reached nirvāṇa. The ascetic answered in one word which means either "it may be so" or "let it be so," shook his head, and walked away on another road. This curious encounter seems like historical fact rather than pious invention. Gautama's first proclamation of his Buddhahood was not heeded.

The Blessed One walked by stages to Benares, about one hundred and thirty miles from Gayā. Four miles north of the city, in the Deer Park at Sārnāth, the five ascetics saw him coming, and resolved not to show more than the minimum courtesy to the backslider who had taken to the easy life. But his charisma was too strong for them, and against their own resolve they saluted him, took his bowl and robe, prepared his seat, and gave him implements with which to wash his feet. The impact of his spiritual presence preceded any word.

The five mendicants called him "Friend Gautama," and he told them not to do so, since he was now a *Tathāgata,* an arhant, a perfectly enlightened one. He declared that he had attained the immortal, that he was going to teach Dharma, and that if they practiced as he taught they would quickly realize it for themselves. The five were dubious, saying that one who quit striving could not have attained the superhuman Dharma. The Buddha denied that he had given up striving, and reasserted his claim. Eventually they admitted that he had never spoken to them in this way before, and agreed to listen willingly and receptively.

Whether the Buddha actually preached on this occasion that discourse the Canon attributes to him is as moot as whether Jesus pronounced the Sermon on the Mount as one discourse on the occasion alleged. The doctrine of the Middle Way, though, is entirely appropriate to the task of persuading the five ascetics that one who had abandoned extreme austerities had not necessarily forsaken the ascetic quest.

The Blessed One condemned two extremes, saying that sensual indulgence is low, vulgar, worldly, unspiritual, and useless, while self-torture is painful, unspiritual, and useless. The Tathāgata has avoided these extremes and so has discovered the Middle Way which leads to enlightenment and nirvāṇa. This Middle Way is the Holy Eightfold Path: (1) right views, (2) right intention, (3) right speech, (4) right action, (5) right livelihood, (6) right effort, (7) right mindfulness, and (8) right concentration.

The Buddha then declared the Four Holy Truths, namely the truth of suffering (birth, decay, illness, death, conjunction with the hated, and separation from the dear—in short the five "appropriating groups" [*skandha*] are suffering); the truth of the source of suffering (thirst or craving for sensual pleasure, for coming to be and for ceasing to be); the truth of the cessation of suffering (when craving ceases entirely through dispassion, renunciation, and nondependence, then suffering ceases); and the truth of the path leading to cessation of suffering (the Holy Eightfold Path). Suffering must be thoroughly understood. The source of suffering must be forsaken. Cessation must be realized, made actual. The Eightfold Path must be cultivated.

Gautama testified that he attained supreme, perfect Enlightenment when and only when he had purified true knowledge and vision of these Four Truths. He had understood suffering, forsaken its cause, realized its cessation, and cultivated the path.

The five bhikṣus welcomed the discourse; and during it, one of them, Kauṇḍinya, acquired the pure Dharma-eye and saw that whatever is subject to arising is subject to cessation. Then the Buddha declared, "Kauṇḍinya has caught on! Kauṇḍinya has caught on!" Kauṇḍinya asked the Buddha for full ordination, which he received with the simple formula, "Come, bhikṣu, the Dharma is well proclaimed. Walk the holy course to the perfect termination of suffering." Thus he became the first member of the Order of Monks (*bhikṣu-saṅgha*).

The other four mendicants took turns begging alms for the group and listening to the Buddha's instruction. Very soon all four attained the Dharma-eye and received admission to the Order.

The Buddha then preached a discourse on the five skandhas, briefly mentioned earlier under the First Truth. Form, feeling, conception, dispositions, and consciousness are each devoid of self (ātman). They are impermanent, and so are subject to suffering. Recognizing this, the saintly disciple overcomes infatuation for the five skandhas and goes to liberation. Hearing this exposition, the five monks were freed from the outflows and thus became arhants.

Commentary on the First Sermon

It is noteworthy that Gautama proclaimed and insisted on his own status. He used two terms current among the ascetic sects—*Victor* and *Tathāgata* ("he who has gone thus, or he who has reached what is really so"). The claim of a hairless ape in bare feet and saffron rags to be omniscient and immortal is virtually incredible to the post-Darwinian world. It was scarcely less preposterous even to professional ascetics in the sixth century B.C. Gautama was unable to convince the stranger whom he met on the road, and eventually prevailed with his old friends by appealing to their knowledge of his responsible character.

Gautama's apparent motive in self-proclamation was not vanity but was to prepare the listener to receive the doctrine. He did not proceed to instruct the five mendicants until they acknowledged his authority and were disposed to assent. His style in the first sermon, as in many later discourses, was didactic rather than demonstrative. He elaborated his points but did not attempt to prove them. The chief guarantee of their truth is that they are the testimony of an Enlightened One. It is assumed that men with keen faculties will find them self-evident. The tone is earnest and exalted, free from sentimentality and hyperbole. Gautama's manifest desire to convince his hearers never shakes his gravity.

Faith in the Buddha as revealer of the Dharma is a first step on the path. Faith is not a substitute for knowledge but is the seed which grows into confirmatory realization. It is willingness to take statements provisionally on trust, confidence in the integrity of a witness, and determination to practice according to instructions. It is not a mental state of boiling zeal but rather of serenity and lucidity. Śāriputra, one of the great disciples, explained that the confidence, like that of a lion, with which he proclaimed the Doctrine came, not from his own superknowledge but from the faith inspired in him as he heard Gautama teach. "I, understanding that Dharma, perfected the quality of faith in the Teacher. And I confessed in my heart: The Blessed One is supremely awakened; the Dharma is well proclaimed by him; the Saṅgha has followed it well."

The fruit of faith is not just progress in wisdom. The saintly disciple who possesses faith in the Three Jewels (Buddha, Dharma, and Saṅgha) may predict for himself that he will never go to rebirth in hell, as an animal, among the ghosts, or in any state of woe. He is a stream-winner, lowest of the four grades of saint, and he is confirmed in the course to enlightenment. The objects of faith are not credal statements (faith is not belief), but holy persons (the Buddha and the Saṅgha) and the Truth (Dharma), of which their statements are just expressions. The decisive efficacy of faith is not that it stimulates its objects to act supernaturally but that it transforms the subject.

The ideas of prediction and confirmation played a conspicuous part even in early Buddhism, and underwent progressive embellishment after the rise of Mahāyāna. The Pali texts often show the Buddha declaring that such and such a disciple has become an arhant, or has become a nonreturner who will sojourn in the highest heavens until he attains nirvāṇa, or has become a once-returner who will attain arhant-ship in his next birth as a man, or has become a stream-winner who is assured that he will not relapse until he attains enlightenment. Confirmation is not an externally imposed predestination, but an irrevocable change in the karmic endowment of the subject. The Buddha, or any arhant, can predict a man's destiny by reading the dispositions in his mind, a feat that is possible through the superknowledges.

Closely related to prediction is certification of attainment. The Buddha's declaration "Kauṇḍinya has caught on!" is the first instance of this formal act. Identifying the saints has always been a problem for the Buddhist devotee, who reveres and makes offerings to them, and whose chief religious authority is their word. Once the sainthood of the Buddha is granted, as it is when one professes the Buddhist faith, it is a convenience to have the Buddha's or an arhant's certification that so and so is a saint of such and such a degree. Like many other early Buddhist institutions, this is a legal solution to a spiritual problem.

What is the Middle Path proclaimed in the First Sermon? It is, like the Greek and Chinese middle way or golden mean, a course of moderation in which the bodily and sensual appetites are fed sufficiently for health rather than indulged or starved. But it comprises much more than this. The Eightfold Path is equivalent to a shorter formula, the Threefold Training, namely morality (right speech, action, and livelihood), wisdom (right views and intention), and concentration (right effort, mindfulness, and concentration). We have already seen all three as strands in the Enlightenment. Morality goes beyond mere self-mortification because it involves intention and the effects of one's acts on others. Wisdom here means intellectual understanding of the Doctrine, of the kind obtained through thinking, study, and meditation. To discipline the intellect is a higher asceticism than merely to hold the breath and keep fasts. Concentration (*samādhi*) is achieved through specific techniques apparently known to Gautama's two teachers but not favored by the five mendicants. It requires not the mortification of the body but the cultivation of psychic skills. The Three Trainings are dependent on one another. "Concentration suffused with morality becomes very fruitful; wisdom suffused with concentration becomes very fruitful; the mind suffused with wisdom is quite freed from the outflows." The Middle Path is not only moderate but comprehensive, engaging the whole man. It is none the less an *askēsis* ("exercise, training, yoga"), and means undertaking a stringent discipline, going against the current of worldly life.

In the Eightfold Path, right action means abstaining from taking life, from taking what is not given, and from sexual misconduct, the three bodily wrong deeds. Right speech means abstaining from lying, slander, abuse, and idle talk, the four vocal wrong deeds. Right livelihood is abstention from occupations that harm living beings, for example selling weapons, liquor, poison, slaves, or livestock; butchering, hunting, fishing; soldiering; fraud, soothsaying, and usury. Right intention is marked by dispassion, benevolence, and aversion to injuring others. Right views means knowledge of the Four Truths. This explains the otherwise abrupt transition in the First Sermon from the Path to the Truths. Another implicit connection is that the Path is the Fourth Truth.

We have already seen that ignorance of the Four Truths is the first of the twelve preconditions, and that knowledge of them is the antidote to transmigratory misery. By realizing them during the third watch, Gautama extinguished the outflows and understood that he had overcome rebirth. Just hearing them, Kauṇḍinya "caught on," had an opening of his religious vision. The Word of the Buddha was no ordinary word, and his Four Truths were no mere worldly theses. These statements were proclaimed to people many of whom believed that the Primal Being produced Speech out of himself, then copulated with her to produce all other creatures. Human speech was considered objectively effective, too; *mantras* ("incantations") were the chief stock in trade of the brāhman ritualist. The propositions of archaic Indian philosophy were just one step removed from mantras. The Holy Truths, like the Great Statements of the Upaniṣads, were not premises for a deductive system but enunciations of *gnōsis* ("saving knowledge") to be meditated upon until the hearer "catches on" and breaks through to another plane of being.

The frequent charge that Buddhism is pessimism because it declares life to be suffering is inaccurate. An early text glowingly praises the blessings of the good householder's life—the company of wise men, honoring the honorable, living in a congenial country, erudition and skill, good manners and speech, looking after one's family, having a peaceful profession, giving alms, doing good deeds, practicing the religion, and becoming immune to worldly sorrow and defilement. The delights of life among the gods are also praised highly, and it is never denied that there is much happiness in the world. It is only asserted that sooner or later one must suffer through separation from dear things, that worldly happiness is yoked to suffering. This observation is a preacher's commonplace, but its acceptance in one form or another is inescapable when bereavement occurs.

Comparative religion suggests two reasons why Gautama gave such prominence to suffering. The first is that suffering is the hallmark of that condition from which salvation is sought. It results from sin (deeds committed out of craving and ignorance, not disobedience as in the Judeo-Christian myth of the Fall), and until the results are seen for what they are, the remedy will not be welcomed. The second reason is that suffering is the essential component of the chief primitive rites of initiation into manhood. The warrior brotherhood tests the initiant by ordeal to see whether he is worthy and to stimulate his martial powers. The shaman guild initiates the neophyte with a ritual dismemberment and other austerities to solemnize his change of status, but even more to effect a transformation of his personality and to endow him with powers. Suffering kills the old self and induces "the second birth." The Buddhist way partakes of both martial and shamanic elements. It is a state of prolonged initiation, lasting until nirvāṇa is attained. The Buddha rejected extreme physical mortification, but in its place he put mental mortification, the contemplation of universal suffering.

Meditation on suffering should result in longing to escape from it, but not through alienation. One ought to cultivate awareness of the suffering of others, and this arouses compassion. Unable to bear others' misery, one tries to lead them out of it. One sees their helplessness and is moved to help. As compassion grows, the desire to harm others withers away. We have noted that, during the Enlightenment, Gautama observed the sufferings of all beings, and that it was the ensuing compassion that moved him to accept Brahmā's request to preach.

The way out of suffering leads, paradoxically and homeopathically, through asceticism, sane and consequential but still painful and hard to accept. One must cut off the roots of suffering, which according to the Second Truth are libidinous drives of all sorts, craving for sensual gratification, hankering for survival, and even the wish for extinction. But how can anyone stop seeking pleasure and continued existence except by desiring death? In Buddhist doctrine, though, death is not release but merely the prelude to rebirth. So the longing to escape from this life through dying ("dis-becoming") is as fatuous as the yearning for another life in suffering.

The Third Truth affirms that there is a happy state free from suffering. When craving ceases, suffering ceases. But is this not tantamount to saying that happiness is a purely negative state consequent upon the extinction of life, an absolute death? And isn't it better to live and suffer than to escape at the price of total annihilation? How can there possibly be positive happiness if all desire is destroyed?

In Buddhism as in Vedānta, the pairs of opposites are not exhaustive. They are contraries rather than true contradictories. To be or become means to be or become in the realm of transmigration. To "dis-become" or "not be" means to pass out of one form (and on to another) within the phenomenal world. In the earliest Indian thought, "being" was the solid, reified state of things, and "nonbeing" was their subtle, unmanifested state. The meaning of the terms changed shortly before the Buddha's time, and "being" came to mean that which endures as against that which changes, the ground in contrast to its modifications. The Buddha is reported to have denied the two widespread extremes of eternalism and annihilation, saying that the Enlightened One, seeing how the world arises, rejects the idea of its nonbeing, and seeing how it perishes, rejects the idea of its being. The Middle Path that avoids these extremes is "dependent arising": "When *A* exists, *B* comes to be." The formula of the twelve preconditions is the usual elaboration of this principle. It is the Middle Way in metaphysics, just as the Eightfold Path is the Middle Way in ethics.

Here "exist" is used in two senses: (1) to occur at one time after arising and before ceasing, and (2) to exist at all times without beginning or end. The second sense is impossible given the Buddhist position that no substance exists apart from its modifications. The Upaniṣad says that the clay is real and the pots are mere modifications created by "naming." The Buddhist says that no clay ever exists apart from particular forms, so the unchanging substratum is unattested and does not exist. Existence in the first sense means manifested existence, and no form of Buddhism has ever denied that commonsense things exist in this relative way, though there has been continual apprehension lest this admission lead people to believe in the second, absolute kind of being.

A wanderer is said to have approached the Buddha and asked a series of questions about ultimate matters. Are the world and souls eternal, noneternal, both, or neither? Are the world and souls infinite in space, finite, both, or neither? Are the soul and the body the same or different? Does the Tathāgata exist after death, not exist, both, or neither? The Buddha in some versions is said to have remained silent (though explaining his silence afterward to a disciple), but in most of the Sūtras he answers definitely that the statement does not fit the case, is not true to fact. But how can it be denied that someone exists without affirming that he does not exist? Perhaps he exists in some ways and in others does not exist. But this, too, is denied, and it would seem to follow then that he neither exists nor does not exist, except that this fourth alternative is denied, too. The answer is that the categories of existence and nonexistence are applicable only in the realm of the conditioned. Nirvāṇa, the unconditioned, transcends them. The fire which "goes out" does not go north, south, east, or west, but home to its unmanifested source. When the fuel of the skandhas is exhausted, the arhant goes home to the unconditioned. He is deep, immeasurable, unfathomable, like the great ocean.

Cessation, it is plain, is transcendence rather than annihilation. Early Buddhism accepted the axiom that being cannot come from nonbeing and cannot go to nonbeing. Thus it ruled out genuine annihilation. Transcendence, though, would not seem to accommodate happiness in any mundane sense. This is congruent with the basic pattern of early Indian negation. Suffering and happiness are paired opposites of finite extension, so to achieve perfect felicity one must rise beyond not only misery but ordinary bliss. The notion of "positive happiness" is a finite, contingent one. But so long as the five skandhas have not dissolved, the arhant lives, and between his enlightenment and his death he certainly is happy. The Canon pictures the Buddha and his liberated disciples vividly as calm, cheerful, spontaneous, even humorous, free from strife, and humane: "Let us live happily, hating none in the midst of men who hate. Let us live happily then, free from disease. Let us live happily then, free from care. Let us live happily then, we who possess nothing. Let us dwell feeding on joy like the Radiant Gods" (Dh. 197–200).

Founding the Saṅgha

After the Second Sermon, there were six arhants in the world, counting Gautama himself. Soon Yasa, a rich merchant's son of Benares, waking up during the night in a state of anxiety, went out to Sārnāth, where the Buddha comforted him and taught him the Dharma suitable for laymen, namely the merit of donation, the moral precepts, heaven, the wretchedness of sensual desires, and the blessings of forsaking them. Then he preached the higher Dharma, the Four Truths, to the young man, who attained "arhant-ship" and then took full ordination as a monk. Later, Yasa's father took the Three Refuges and thus became the first lay devotee (*upāsaka*) in the strict sense; the two merchants at Bodhgayā had not been able to take refuge in the Saṅgha since it did not yet exist. His mother and sisters took the Three Refuges and became the first female devotees (*upāsikā*). Yasa's friends came, listened to the Buddha, took ordination, and became free from the outflows until there were sixty-one arhants in the world.

Throughout its history, Buddhism has appealed particularly to the merchant class, especially those engaged in the caravan trade and in large-scale finance. Mercantile ideas of accountability and responsibility underlie the doctrines of merit and karma. A world view in which fortune is rational, the regular result of specific acts, appeals to enterprising men who would rather shape their destiny than just let fate happen to them. And the doctrine of the conservation of virtue reassures them that even if they fail in business they can succeed in religion.

The Buddhist Community (Saṅgha) consisted of four assemblies: monks, nuns, laymen, and laywomen. The rites of entry into these assemblies are both legal and sacramental in character, hence the great importance that the Vinaya attaches to their institution. Going for refuge is a formal act of submitting to the authority and claiming the protection of a powerful patron, whether a man or a god. The formula is uttered three times to make it solemn and magico-legally binding. Those and only those who take refuge in Buddha, Dharma, and Saṅgha are Buddhists. Though it has been said that the monastics are the only true Buddhists, this is not the case. All who have taken the Refuges belong. The commitment is formal and definite. Though it does not require credal assent to tenets such as the Four Truths, it does constitute a profession of faith in the Buddha's wisdom, the truth of his teaching, and the worthiness of the Saṅgha.

When the cadre of sixty enlightened monks was consolidated, the Buddha sent them out as missionaries, charging them to travel and proclaim the Dharma for the benefit of the many, out of compassion for the world, for the welfare of gods and men. Beings with keen faculties would attain liberation if and only if they heard the doctrine.

The historic success of Buddhism stems from its concern for the many, regardless of race, caste, class, or sex. Compassion is not just feeling the suffering of others, but acting to alleviate it, and the foremost act is "Dharma-donation." The Brāhmanical schools kept their teachings as secret as possible, and their teachers retained personal control over the students. The Buddhists broadcast their message to the multitudes, aiming it specifically, though, to those most ready to receive it. The good Dharma-preacher uses his divine eye (or lacking that, the science of character analysis) to discern whether people are dull, medium, or keen minded, and to adapt the teaching to the hearer's capacity. In the Quaker phrase, he "speaks to the condition" of his audience.

The missionary aims not only to proclaim his doctrine but to communicate it.

Only Buddhas attain enlightenment without receiving the gift of the Dharma from another, and even they, according to later theory, heard it many lives ago from a former Buddha. Thus no one works out his own salvation unaided: "You yourself must make an effort. The Buddhas, for their part, are the revealers" (Dh. 276). The later disputes over self-power versus other-power (see pp. 166, 206 ff., 239) concern the price of salvation, and do not deny that it takes two parties for anyone to achieve it. Every form of Buddhism has held that guides are necessary; and though the Buddhas are the highest guides, the other saints and even some worldlings perform the office.

The sixty missionaries were soon so successful that many converts came long distances to receive ordination. The Buddha noted the hardship this caused them, and so granted his monks permission to confer ordination themselves wherever they went. This made the Saṅgha self-propagating and enabled it to spread far beyond the area within which the Buddha or any pontiff could have exercised personal control. Even during his lifetime, Gautama entrusted his Community with management of its own affairs, serving as lawmaker when his disciples consulted him on problems but otherwise not imposing his authority. By the time of his decease, the Saṅgha was consolidated as a republican society, a loose federation of little democracies bound together by a common code, a common oral tradition, and the constant coming and going of itinerant monks.

Śākyamuni spent the first three-month rainy season at Sārnāth, near Benares. This summer monsoon retreat became an institution and is observed to the present day in Theravāda countries. After the rains he returned to Uruvelā, where he had practiced austerities. The Vinaya relates that there he encountered and converted three brothers of the Kāśyapa clan who with their hundreds of disciples belonged to the Jaṭila sect of Brāhmanic ascetics.

This tale shows how Buddhism grew not merely through individual conversions but by incorporating whole sects. It is remarkable that all the early converts speedily became arhants. In later centuries Buddhists attributed this to the superior capacities of people born in the auspicious age when a Buddha was alive. It is at least as likely that many of the reported attainments are just pious exaggeration, for example, that of the thousand ex-Jaṭilas, all of whom are said to have become arhants. Even so, the arhant-ship of individual famous disciples is uncontested in the tradition. Doubtless Gautama's personal charisma enormously facilitated realization. Furthermore, his good news burst like a sudden light in a milieu thronging with expectant seekers. The fuel was dry and ready for the spark.

The Buddha went on to Rājagṛha, capital of Magadha, where he was greeted by King Bimbisāra and a large crowd. The king entertained him and donated the Bamboo Grove park just outside the northern gates of the city. Soon Śāriputra of Nālandā, about ten miles north of Rājagṛha, and his friend Maudgalyāyana were converted. They became the two chief disciples, Śāriputra being foremost in wisdom, and Maudalyāyana foremost in magic powers. They died before the Buddha did, and relics said to be theirs are now enshrined in a new temple on the ancient site at Sāñcī. Among other famous disciples there was Mahākāśyapa, foremost of those who keep the ascetic rules, who shortly after the Buddha's decease convened the Council of Rājagṛha and superintended the recitation of the Sūtras. Subhūti, foremost among those who dwell in peace, supreme in practicing the samādhi of emptiness and foremost among those worthy of offerings, attained arhant-ship by meditating on friendly love (maitrī). Kātyāyana, a brāhman and court priest from Avantī in Western India, was sent by his king on a mission to the Buddha, who sent him back as a bhikṣu and arhant to spread the Dharma in Avantī. He was the father of Buddhist exegesis, known as "foremost of those who analyze at length what the Buddha has stated concisely." Upāli, the barber of Kapilavastu, became "foremost among those who keep the Vinaya," which he recited at the First Council. Tradition says that Gautama's own son, Rāhula, received ordination and became an arhant. He was considered foremost among those who love to train.

Gautama's cousin Ānanda became a monk and was his favorite disciple and constant attendant for the last twenty years of his life. He figures often in the account of the Buddha's last weeks and was present at his death. Ānanda alone among the great disciples had not become an arhant, so Mahākāśyapa excluded him from the First Council, admitting him after he had retired and overnight achieved extinction of the outflows. His exceptional memory enabled him, it is said, to recite accurately the dialogs of the Buddha which then composed the *Sūtra Piṭaka* ("Collection"; literally, "Basket").

The Order of Nuns is said to have been instituted by the Buddha at Ānanda's repeated plea. Gautama's foster mother Prajāpatī and her attendants became its first members. Queen Kṣemā, wife of King Bimbisāra, was converted and became a prominent nun. Despite the example of such wise and saintly ladies, the female order never became nearly so important as the male one.

The early lay converts include a good array of kings, princes, and rich merchants. Of the latter, Anāthapiṇḍaka donated the land for the famous Jetavana monastery at Śrāvastī. Two wealthy laywomen also donated to the Saṅgha, the courtesan Amrapālī giving her garden at Vaiśālī and the matron Viśākhā giving land for a monastery in Śrāvastī. Thus even during the Buddha's lifetime his Saṅgha became a wealthy landowner.

The Parinirvāṇa

For forty-five years the Buddha journeyed around the central Gangetic plain, staying in the Saṅgha's parks, receiving all callers—śramaṇas, brāhmans, princes, and commoners—and answering their questions, converting the unconverted, and instructing the converts.

In his seventy-ninth year, Gautama set out on his last journey. He left

Rājagṛha and moved by stages north and west until he reached Vaiśālī, where he fell seriously ill. The *Sūtra of the Great Decease* says that he told Ānanda that through magic powers he could stay alive for a *kalpa* ("aeon, world-period"), but Ānanda failed to request him to do so. Then Māra approached and told Gautama that it was time for him to attain final nirvāṇa. The Buddha agreed, saying, "Trouble not, Evil One. Very soon the Tathāgata's parinirvāṇa will take place. After three months he will enter parinirvāṇa."

These episodes betray the notions of a later age puzzled by the seeming failure of the deceased master to avert his own death. Control of one's lifespan is a yogic power, and even today India and the Buddhist world are full of reports about holy men who have lived well beyond a hundred years. Great holy men similarly can predict or determine the date of their death.

The Tathāgata's last meal was at the home of Cunda the smith. After eating a quantity of pork (later commentators say mushrooms), he became very sick, blood flowed, and he suffered sharp dysentery pains. He bore it calmly, arose and went to Kuśinagara, where he lay down between two śāla trees. There he received the wanderer Subhadra, to whom he recommended the Holy Eightfold Path. Ānanda then received this last convert into the Saṅgha.

The dying Buddha asked the assembled monks three times whether they had any last doubts or questions, but all kept silent. So the Blessed One delivered his last exhortation: "Conditioned things are perishable by nature. Diligently seek realization." Then he entered the first dhyāna and ascended the trance states up to the fourth, from which he passed into parinirvāṇa.

The legend says that earthquakes and thunder marked the moment of death. Brahmā and Śakra recited stanzas, and the monks (except the arhants) burst into lamentation until Anuruddha reminded them that doing so was not in keeping with the Buddha's teaching.

The people of Kuśinagara came the next day and held a six-day wake for the Blessed One. They danced, sang, made music, and offered garlands and scents. The body was wrapped in alternate layers of cloth and cotton wool. On the seventh day, eight chiefs of the Mallas carried the bier in the north gate and out the east gate of the town to a tribal shrine. There they cremated the body.

When they asked Ānanda how the remains of the Tathāgata should be treated, he replied, "Like those of a king of kings. Cremate the body, and build a mound [*stūpa*] at the crossroads to enshrine the relics."

Simple worshippers believe that the physical relics radiate a spiritual force. In fact the sense of physical continuity evokes such a power in the devotee's mind. But Gautama is reported to have said, "What is there in seeing this wretched body? Whoever sees Dharma sees me; whoever sees me sees Dharma." The immortality of the Buddha is that he is immanent in his Word.

3.

Development of Indian Buddhism

Formation of the Canon

Just before the Buddha died, he reportedly told his followers that thereafter the Dharma would be their leader. The early arhants considered Gautama's words the primary source of Dharma and Vinaya, and took great pains to formulate and transmit his teachings accurately. Nonetheless, no ungarnished collection of his sayings has survived. The versions of the Canon preserved in Pali, Sanskrit, Chinese, and Tibetan are sectarian variants of a corpus that grew and crystalized during three centuries of oral transmission.

The Buddhist chronicles present an anachronistic and idealized story of the First Council, held at Rājagṛha during the three-month monsoon retreat after the Parinirvāṇa. Mahākāśyapa, it is said, first questioned Upāli, who stated when and under what circumstances the Buddha promulgated each rule of the Vinaya. Textual criticism, though, shows that while some of the material in the Vinayas of the various Hīnayāna ("Small Vehicle or Course") sects may go back to the first generation of disciples, the literary form and much of the content is centuries later.

Ānanda is said to have recited in order each of the five *Nikāyas* (also called *Āgamas*) in the *Sūtra Piṭaka* ("Basket of Discourses"). Four Nikāyas are recognized by all the early sects: The Long (*Dīgha*), the Medium (*Majjhima*), the Connected (*Saṃyutta*), and the Item-More (*Aṅguttara*) *Nikāya.* But the Little (*Khuddaka*) Nikāya as a collection is found only in Pali and not in the Chinese translations, even though many of its texts (such as the *Dhammapada*) exist in Chinese as separate works or parts of other Āgamas.

The canonical texts are chiefly in prose, except for stanzas interspersed through the first four Nikāyas and the anthologies of verse (Dhammapada, Sutta-nipāta, and so on) in the fifth Nikāya. In the prose texts, the early disciples seem to have been concerned with the substantive content rather than with the exact words. Everyone was allowed to recite the scriptures in his own dialect. We do not know precisely what language the Buddha spoke, but it was probably the precursor of the Māgadhī dialect in which most of Aśoka's inscriptions are couched. The complete Canon of the Theravāda sect has been preserved in Pali, a vernacular descended from Sanskrit and probably spoken in West India from where it was taken to Ceylon. Tradition says that the Pali Canon was written down in Ceylon during the first century B.C. Probably the Canon was reduced to writing in North India during the second century B.C.

Sectarian bias undoubtedly has occasioned distortions, additions, and omissions. Nevertheless, a large fund is common to all versions, and the Saṅgha seems from the first to have striven to exclude spurious texts and to maintain purity of transmission.

Strictness in preserving the essential kernel, and liberty to expand, vary, and embellish the expression, characterize Buddhist attitudes through the ages toward not only texts but art, ritual, discipline, and doctrine. The perennial difficulty lies in distinguishing the kernel from its embodiment. The Buddha is said to have told Ānanda that if the Saṅgha wished it might revoke the minor rules; but Ānanda forgot to ask which rules were minor, so the First Council, it is said, decided to retain everything in the Vinaya.

The third collection in the Pali Canon is the *Abhidhamma* (Skt. Abhidharma) *Piṭaka.* It consists of seven scholastic works, and is peculiar to the Theravāda school. Other sects had their own Abhidharma literatures. None of these texts is the word of the Buddha. They are the compositions of schoolmen in later centuries.

Early Schisms and Sects

The early teaching admits that a layman can attain the first three degrees of sainthood (stream-winner, once-returner, and nonreturner); but whether he could become an arhant was a disputed point. The Buddha reportedly declared that he took no categorical stand, that with the layman as with the monk it is conduct that counts. The Sūtras list twenty upāsakas who attained the highest goal without ever becoming monks. Their case, though, is rarer than that of monks becoming arhants, and the household life is not considered propitious for the highest attainment.

The arhant monks formed an elite guild in the early Community and alienated many other monks and laymen by insisting that they alone knew the True Dharma and were qualified to pronounce on the correctness of views and the holiness of others. Some opposed this monopoly by declaring that a householder could become an arhant and keep his lay status. And some opponents belittled the arhants, maintained that the arhant was liable to relapse, and contradicted claims that he was in every way omnipotent and omniscient. Even the Buddha was not accorded such powers in the early teaching. At the same period, there was a universal tendency to attribute more and more extraordinary powers to the Buddha, such as the ability to live for a whole kalpa, and knowledge of all facts.

During the second century A.N. (after the Nirvāṇa), the Community split into two sects, the *Sthaviras* (Pali *Thera,* "Elders") and the *Mahāsaṅghikas* ("Great Assembly-ites"). The Elders claimed to be conservative, but in fact distorted the primitive teaching considerably by aggrandizing themselves and the Buddha. The Mahāsaṅghikas admitted upāsakas and non-arhant monks to their meetings, and were sensitive to popular religious values and aspirations.

They were progressive innovators; two out of three basic strands in the Mahāyāna are of Mahāsaṅghika origin (see p. 49). Yet in some ways they remained truer to the primitive teaching than did the Elders. They kept the open, permissive structure as against the bureaucratic exclusivism of the Sthaviras. And they refused to gild the lotus of arhant-ship. But they carried the transfiguration of the Buddha much further than the Sthaviras did, holding that he is supermundane and perfectly pure. His body is infinite, his power is boundless, and his life is endless. He educates living beings tirelessly, awakening pure faith in them. Furthermore, apparition-bodies of the Buddha appear and act in different world-realms at the same time.

Half a dozen subsects came out of the Mahāsaṅghikas, partly over doctrinal disputes and partly through geographic separation.

The Sthaviras underwent another major schism about two hundred years A.N. The schismatics were *Pudgalavādins* ("Personalists"), who asserted that there exists a person (*pudgala*) who is neither identical with the five skandhas nor different from them, but who nonetheless knows, transmigrates, and enters nirvāṇa. They said, on the other hand, that the factors (*skandhas*) that constitute the phenomenal person are mere designations, not real substances. The Sūtras contain many statements that can be cited in support of these views. The pudgala of the Personalists is rather like the *vijñāna* ("consciousness") that transmigrates and enters nirvāṇa according to the early teaching. Furthermore, the canonical expositions of the no-self or no-soul (*nairātmya*) doctrine are ambiguous. They deny that any one of the skandhas is the ātman, and so conclude that the five taken together are not the ātman.

The Personalists said that the pudgala is to the skandhas as fire is to the fuel, neither identical nor different. If it were other than the skandhas, it would be eternal and unconditioned, which is a heretical view. If it were the same as the skandhas, it would undergo annihilation, also a heretical view.

The Abhidharma masters of the Sthavira schools surely deviated from the early teaching when they declared that the elements (*dharmas*) are real things (*vastu*) or substances (*dravya*), while the person is just a designation. The Personalists denied that either dharmas or pudgalas are real things, while affirming that both exist as designations, that is, as objects of commonsense knowledge and statements. This is more explicit than, but consonant with, the Sūtras' teaching. It is also the position that Mahāyāna later took.

The Personalists maintained that nirvāṇa is neither really the same as, nor really distinct from, phenomena (*dharmas*). If the person is neither the same as, nor other than, the elements, then its cessation must be neither the same nor different. Saṃsāra, also, is to nirvāṇa as the fuel is to the fire. It would be going rather far to make an active principle out of nirvāṇa, even for the Personalists, but this is just what the Vijñānavādins (see p. 70) later did. The Sthavira tradition emphasized the utter transcendence of nirvāṇa, and refused to concede that it is immanent in saṃsāra even when the Sūtras used symbols for immanence such as the fire and the ocean. The Tathāgata who dies is like the fire that goes out. Gautama's hearers believed that fire is an indestructible element latent in every bright or warm thing, but especially in fuel. It alternates between manifestation and "going home" to its occult source. In the Vedas and Brāhmaṇas, the ocean is the reservoir from which the streams of differentiated existence proceed and to which they revert when the liberated one merges back. So the Tathāgata, residing in this nirvāṇa-realm, is subtler than the subtlest (like fire) and greater than the greatest (like the ocean). These are precisely the predicates of the ātman and brahman in the Upaniṣads. The Personalists were more cautious than the Upaniṣads in asserting immanence, but they kept alive this aspect of the early ontology and prepared the way for Mahāyāna doctrines such as that all living beings are endowed with suchness and with Buddha-nature. As a sect they thrived for over a thousand years.

This seemingly obscure philosophical dispute really has vital relevance to a cardinal religious issue: the value to be placed upon this world. Buddhism, like Christianity, has passed its centuries in a continual quandary on this point. If a spiritual reality dwells in and suffuses this world, then worldly and secular activities such as raising a family and scientific research have inherent worth. But if the worldly and the spiritual realms are mutually alien and exclusive, then profane things and activities have no intrinsic value and are significant only insofar as they contribute to escape from the profane realm into the spiritual. Christianity sided wholeheartedly neither with the orthodox Jewish affirmation nor with the Gnostic rejection of this world. Buddhism similarly preferred an enigmatic Middle Way against the easy-to-understand dead-end extremes of mere worldliness and mere otherworldliness.

A third schism rent the Sthavira school at the Council of Pāṭaliputra, about 250 B.C. The two factions were called *Sarvāstivādins* ("All-is-ists") and *Vibhajyavādins* ("Distinctionists"). The chief Sarvāstivādin thesis is that past and future things really exist, as do present things.

The Council of Pāṭaliputra decided against the Sarvāstivādins, some of whom migrated west and north. They established a strong center in Kashmir which flourished for a thousand years. They came to dominate the cities on the northern branch of the trade route between China and the West. From there, they entered China and exerted a powerful influence.

It is doubtful whether the Sarvāstivādin theories about time and being are religiously important. This school did, however, nourish a doctrine that became one cornerstone of the Mahāyāna: the perfections. The *bodhisattva,* they said, fulfils six perfections: donation, morality, patience, vigor, meditation, and wisdom. Each of these virtues is frequently commended in the Sūtras, but they become perfections only when carried to the utmost extreme. The Jātaka tales, extracanonical but attested in the art of the second century B.C., relate how Gautama in his former lives accomplished each perfection. These popular tales urged the listener to imitate the Bodhisattva, but did not tell him to become a bodhisattva, a step that was taken by early Mahāyāna.

About 350 A.N. the Sautrāntikas split off from the Sarvāstivādins. They denied that past and future dharmas really exist, holding that, if this were true, conditioned things would exist forever, which is not so. The Sarvāstivādins held that three unconditioned dharmas exist, namely space, nirvāṇa, and non-cognizant cessation. This view was at variance with the early teaching. The Sautrāntikas, though, declared that these entities were not real dharmas but just absences. Space is absence of the touchable, and nirvāṇa is absence of dispositions toward becoming. This ingenious and drastic thesis does as much violence to the early "neither-nor" position as does the Sarvāstivādin assertion that nirvāṇa is a dharma ("force-factor, element, basic thing"). The Sūtras do declare that there is an unborn, unbecome, unmade, and unconditioned. They also say that nirvāṇa is the destruction of old age and death, and that the stopping of becoming is nirvāṇa. Plainly, the Sūtras are inconsistent, and the Sarvāstivādins and Sautrāntikas chose opposing one-sided consistencies.

The Sautrāntikas are so called because they denied that Abhidharma has scriptural authority and only acknowledged the *Sūtrāntas* (= Sūtras). Nonetheless they contributed much to the development of Abhidharma thought, and furnished the Mahāyāna both with critiques of Sarvāstivāda and with key concepts such as that of "seeds" that carry the effects of deeds latent in the personality stream until their time comes, and pure force-factors (dharmas) innate even in worldlings and never completely annihilated.

To return to the Council of Pāṭaliputra, the Vibhajyavādins were united chiefly by their opposition to the Sarvāstivādins, and soon came apart into sects. One of these, the Mahīśāsakas, was situated in the Narbada Valley (that is, between Sāñcī and Ajanta), from where it spread south to the Deccan and coastal Andhra. While the sect persisted until the fifth century A.D., its monks had over the centuries taken to Mahāyāna and gradually lost their sectarian tenets.

The Dharmaguptakas separated from the Mahīśāsakas quite early, and apparently were located chiefly in North-West India and Serindia (Central Asia). They became influential in China, where large portions of their Canon are extant. They revered Maudgalyāyana, "foremost in magic powers" (p. 33), and were expert in the art of incantation. In this respect they developed a practice that plays a very minor part in the Pali Sūtras, but which burgeoned with the rise of Tantrism.

An archaic group of Vibhajyavādins belonging to or closely affiliated with the Mahīśāsakas became established in Ceylon, at the Great Monastery of Anurādhapura, about 240 B.C. They had no special sectarian name, but called themselves simply *Theravādins* ("Those Who Hold the Teachings of the Elders or Sthaviras"). Their Abhidharma, though archaic, includes considerable sectarian innovation beyond the doctrines of the *Sūtra Piṭaka.* For most of the second century B.C., Ceylon was ruled by the non-Buddhist Tamils, and the Theravādins were cut off from developments in India. By the time Ceylon became independent again, its Buddhism was confirmed in the archaistic cast that it has since retained.

The tables of sect names, deceptively like grammatical paradigms, convey an impression of orderliness and exclusiveness which is contrary to fact. It is true that bhikṣus belonged to the ordination lineages of one or another sect, but they were free to study the doctrines of the other schools, and even to adopt specific tenets of rival schools without incurring expulsion from their own group. Inscriptions show that monasteries "belonged" to specific sects, but members of different schools frequently lived side by side in the same vihāra, and traveling bhikṣus were given temporary shelter in the cloisters of all persuasions.

Aśoka

In 260 B.C., Aśoka, third Emperor of the Maurya dynasty, attacked and conquered Kaliṅga (the Orissa coast), the only part of India that had rejected Maurya suzerainty. The bloodshed and destruction were extensive, and the emperor was filled with remorse. He began to study the Dharma, went on pilgrimage to Bodhgayā, took the Three Refuges, and gave up the royal pastime of hunting because it infringed the first precept (not to take life). He visited the bhikṣus frequently, received instruction, and spent some time in retreat as a lay brother.

Five years after attacking Kaliṅga, Aśoka again took bold action, but this time to proclaim the policy of Dharma-conquest which he now preferred to military conquest. He had a series of edicts engraved on rocks and polished stone pillars throughout his empire, and instructed his officials to read them to the public on festival days. These inscriptions are the earliest surviving compositions by a Buddhist layman, and they serve as a reminder that though the householder Dharma does not occupy much space in the Canon compiled by the monks, it loomed large in the life of ancient India.

Aśoka proclaims his devotion to the Three Jewels, yet assumes the prerogative of advising the bhikṣu-saṅgha on what texts to study, and of expelling schism-causers, whom he required to give up the saffron robe, to adopt the layman's white garments, and to live outside the monasteries. The emperor's favor enriched the Saṅgha and attracted multitudes of opportunist recruits, whom the regular monks accused of introducing non-Buddhist doctrines. It has been truly remarked that the survival and prosperity of Buddhism have usually depended on its ability to enlist the support of rulers. The twin of this blessing, though, is that the thistles grow with the wheat, and the king is obliged to weed the crop that he has sown.

The emperor's motive in adopting Buddhism was a blend of personal conviction and political astuteness. In the plain and personal style of the Edicts, sincere concern for the welfare of his subjects and his neighbors' subjects shows through more clearly than in any other royal pronouncements of the ancient world. He could afford to give up warfare as a major policy instrument; he was undisputed master of South Asia, and enjoyed peaceful relations with Persia, his only strong neighbor. But his problem was to consolidate a heterogeneous assortment of tribes and peoples into one cultural community. To achieve this end, he sought an ideological common denominator, and utilized all the available means of communication to propagate it.

The Dharma commended in the Edicts is the common core of the brāhmaṇa and śramaṇa traditions, and not just the Dharma of the Buddha. Aśoka proclaimed that he honored and made gifts to ascetics and householders of all sects. His aim, he said, was growth of the essence in all sects, which means not praising one's own and not disparaging others' sects. He recommended that the different schools listen to and learn from each other. Dharma to him meant chiefly the first four perfections: donation, morality, patience (tolerance), and vigor. He says nothing about meditation or wisdom, which of course would not normally have been expounded to the laity. The Edicts encourage: willing obedience and honor to one's parents, teachers, and other elders; liberality to relatives, acquaintances, and men of religion; abstention from killing animals whether for food or in sacrifice; moderation in spending and accumulating wealth; and kindness to serfs and servants. Among the mental qualities commended are self-control, gratitude, devotion, compassion, and truthfulness.

The Dharma of the Edicts is not just humanistic morality. Aśoka claimed that he had caused gods to mingle with men in India as they had never done before. This may mean that, by fostering offerings to holy men and the devatās and by promoting Dharma, he had propitiated the spirits and drawn them down to the altars and homes of his people. He sponsored religious shows in which the people saw models of the paradises with images of the gods. They were told that through zeal in Dharma they could attain life in those heavens. And all the virtues were extolled as producing merit, which leads to rebirth in the deva-worlds. Legend says that Aśoka built 84,000 stūpas, but even the more modest tally of history and archaeology abundantly testifies that worship ranked as highly as ethical conduct in the emperor's religion.

One Edict says that in 256 and 255 B.C. Aśoka sent Dharma-envoys to the Greek rulers of Syria, Egypt, Macedonia, Cyrene, and Epyrus, as well as to the Tamils in South India. His missionaries left no traceable impression on the Mediterranean world, but succeeded to some degree closer to home. A bilingual Greek-Aramaic inscription of Aśoka at Kandahār in Afghanistan records the measures he had taken to "make men more pious," and concludes, "Acting in this way, during their present life and in their future existence they will live better and more happily together in all things."

Religious Life in the Early Centuries

The Canon furnishes evidence for the practices of the community, lay as well as monastic, during the century after Aśoka's death. The Pali Vinaya (which is still in theory the rule in Theravāda monasteries, though large parts of it have fallen into disuse), prescribes the correct life for the monk, and describes, in telling the origin of each rule, the colorful abuses against which the Order had to protect itself. Areas in which the Saṅgha was well established were divided into districts, each approximately twenty miles square. Each district had one *uposatha* ("observance") hall, at which all monks resident within the district were required to assemble on the last day of each half-month for recitation of the *Pātimokkha* ("Rules of Discipline"). This code consists of five classes of offense, plus rules of deportment and some procedural principles. Four offenses warrant permanent expulsion: fornication, theft, killing a human being, and falsely claiming spiritual attainments.

Thirteen offenses require a formal meeting of the Saṅgha chapter consisting of at least twenty monks, and are punished with probation. The first five of these concern sex: intentional ejaculation, touching a woman or speaking suggestively to her, urging a woman to earn merit by yielding to a man of religion, and serving as a go-between. Two rules deal with the prescribed size and the approved site of monks' dwellings. Six rules pertain to concord in the Order. For example, it is an offense to harrass a fellow monk by false accusations of an offense that merits expulsion, or to support such an accusation with misleading testimony. And it is an offense to persist in causing discord within the Saṅgha after the assembly has three times formally warned the culprit to desist.

Thirty offenses require expiation and forfeiture of the article involved. They deal mainly with robes, alms bowls, and seat rugs.

Ninety-two offenses require expiation. The list is quite miscellaneous: lying, abuse, slander, stealing another bhikṣu's sleeping space, taking more than one meal at a public rest house, sporting in the water, or eavesdropping while other monks quarrel. It is prohibited to dig the ground, to destroy any vegetable, or to sprinkle water with living creatures in it. Thus the monk could not practice agriculture. These rules, ostensibly to protect worms and bugs, also safeguarded the monk against lapsing into peasanthood and neglecting the Dharma. Another group of rules prohibits the monk (except for good cause) from going near an army drawn up for battle, from staying with an army more than two or three nights, and from watching the troops on parade. The idea seems to be that the monk should not be an accessory to bloodshed. The prohibitions were doubtless also intended to prevent him from engaging in espionage or diplomatic intrigue.

Taking animal life deliberately does not warrant expulsion, as does killing a human being, but merely expiation. The monk must not even drink water that contains living things. But eating meat is not forbidden in the *Pātimokkha*, though drinking liquor is an offense to be expiated.

Telling a nonmonk that oneself or another monk has extraordinary spiritual powers, even when it is true, is an expiable offense, and so is telling a nonmonk that a bhikṣu has committed a grave offense. On the other hand, every monk is duty-bound to inform the assembly of any serious transgression committed by a fellow monk. Since the Vinaya provides formal procedures for judging the accused and prescribing penance, and since an unconfessed and unexpiated sin is considered an affliction that increases the longer it goes unabsolved, the informer was doing the accused a kindness.

Some of the seventy-five rules of deportment relate to the conduct of the monk while going on his begging rounds among the laymen's homes, receiving alms, eating, and excreting. Sixteen rules forbid the monk to preach Dharma to a monk or layman whose deportment is disrespectful.

The over-all purpose of the rules of deportment is to render the monk worthy of reverence and of offerings, and to ensure that he receives the formal respect to which he is entitled. The bhikṣu must himself maintain impeccable conduct, and allow the laity to choose their response. If they revile him, he suffers it with gentle dignity. If they behave like pigs, he withholds the pearls of the Dharma. The good monk is indifferent to success and failure, gain and loss.

In themselves the rules of deportment seem trivial and quaint. The Saṅgha, though, accepted recruits from all social classes and peoples. It had to refine vulgar boys and civilize uncouth barbarians. Etiquette does not suffice, of course, but it is a necessary part of the complete discipline through which character is shaped, good habits built, and external observances converted into inner discipline.

A noteworthy feature of the Vinaya rules is that they are utterly free from prerational tabus of the sort so common in the Brāhmanical and Hebrew lawbooks. There is no idea that certain foods are impure, or that bodily wastes pollute spiritually, or that certain acts or objects are lucky or unlucky. The authors of the Vinaya certainly thought that spirits and gods exist, yet no place is given to tabu plants and animals associated with particular divinities, a department in which Classical Hinduism rivals the cults of the ancient Near East. Nevertheless, the two dominant ethical concerns of the code—not taking life, and continence—are carried to extremes not justifiable on humanistic and pragmatic grounds. The implicit premises are that life breath (or lifeblood) and semen are tabu. Animal sacrifice offers up the sacred life substance, while nonviolence (*ahiṃsā*) earns merit by saving life, and then devotes the merit to holy objectives, while ascetic continence saves the force of Eros and applies it to spiritual goals.

The Vinaya does not see the monk as working out his own salvation unaided, like the self-made man of nineteenth-century capitalist folklore. Each monk is his brother's keeper; and, when the ordinand joins the Saṅgha, he surrenders some liberties and submits to the collective authority of the Community. Several disciplinary procedures are laid down for reducing the obstinate and the wayward to conformity.

The discipline presupposes a high degree of earnestness and integrity. It will work only if most candidates enter voluntarily and in good faith. For this reason, full ordination is not granted to anyone under twenty years of age. Eight years, though, is the minimum age for the novitiate ordination, which even adult candidates must undergo before proceeding to full ordination. In the "going forth" ceremony, the ordinand is invested with the saffron robes, has his head shaven, and takes the Three Refuges and the ten precepts, namely to abstain from: (1) taking life, (2) taking what is not given, (3) sexual misconduct, (4) lying, (5) drinking liquor, (6) eating after noon, (7) watching dancing, singing, and shows, (8) adorning himself with garlands, perfumes, and ointments, (9) using a high bed, and (10) receiving gold and silver. He is then a novice, and has left the household life. If he is under twenty, he must live with his preceptor until he comes of age. The preceptor must have passed ten years since his full ordination, and must be of good character and competent. The novice also receives instruction from a tutor.

Ordination is conferred by an assembly of at least ten bhikṣus. The candidate accompanied by his tutor comes before the president of the assembly, whom he petitions for admission to the order. Then he retires to the foot of the assembly, his alms bowl strapped onto his back, and his tutors examine him to ascertain that he has his bowl, under robe, upper robe, and mantle. Then the tutor asks him in the hearing of the whole assembly whether he is free from certain diseases and whether he is a free human male, debtless, exempt from military service, furnished with his parents' permission, and at least twenty years of age. The candidate is then made to go forward, kneel, and ask the assembly for ordination. The assembly signifies assent by silence, so the candidate stands up, and the tutors put him through the interrogation again. One of the tutors reports that the candidate desires ordination, that he is free from disqualifications, and that he has a bowl and a set of robes, that he asks for ordination, and that the assembly grants ordination. If any approve, let them be silent. If anyone objects, let him speak. When the assembly keeps silent through the third repetition of this proclamation, the two tutors announce to the president that the candidate has received ordination. The date and hour are then noted, since seniority in the order commences from the time of ordination. The new monk is given an exhortation, in which he is told that henceforth his four reliances are to be on alms for food, on old rags for clothing, on the shade of a tree for shelter, and on cow's urine for medicine. Actual monastic life is usually much less austere; the laity prepare good food for the monks, and donate new robes annually just after the rainy season retreat.

From very early indeed, the Community lived in residences (*vihāra*) made of wood with thatched roofs. About 200 B.C. they began to receive rock-cut vihāras from wealthy donors, in which the features of the wooden prototypes —pillars, joists, and rafters—were imitated in stone. Around the same time, vihāras of fired brick came into general use. Doubtless humble dwellings of wood and thatch, like the typical village vihāra in modern Ceylon, continued to outnumber the imposing brick and stone ones that survive for archaeological study. The remains of the brick residences at Sāñcī, Sārnāth, and Nālandā, and their rock-cut counterparts at Kārlā and Ajantā, exhibit a common plan. Four rows of cells, each eight to ten feet square, a half dozen or more cells to a row, surround a central courtyard which was part of the cave in the rock-cut *vihāras* and was probably enclosed with thatch or a canopy in the brick ones. The cells contained one or two brick or stone benches, which were covered with rugs and used both as seats and as beds, like modern Indian benches. Apparently only elders and perhaps their personal attendants lived in the cells; the junior monks and novices slept in the central courtyard, which also served as a classroom and a refectory.

Some bhikṣus evidently lived alone in huts, either near a village or deep in the jungle. The Vinaya specifies the maximum size for such huts. Solitary residence was more favorable for meditation and the practice of austerities than was the communal life of the larger vihāras, where the daily routine comprised many activities other than meditation, and where most bhikṣus did not practice more than the mild austerity required by the Vinaya.

The main outlines of the daily monastic routine seem to have changed little through the centuries in India, and to have undergone no major changes in China. The Ceylonese commentator Buddhaghosa in the fourth century A.D. based his account of the Buddha's daily habits on the standard monastic routine. The Buddha, he says, got up at daybreak, rinsed his mouth and went to the toilet, and sat quietly until it was time to go on the begging rounds (about 8 or 9 A.M. nowadays in Theravāda countries), when he put on his robes, took his bowl, and entered the village or town for alms. The bhikṣu's residence was supposed to be near enough to a village that he could easily go there to beg, and far enough away that he would not be distracted by noise and company. The Buddha, says Buddhaghosa, was usually received with honor by householders who vied to invite him and his companions to lunch. They would seat him, and place food reverently in his bowl. Then when he had eaten, he would discourse on Dharma to his hosts. Returning to the monastery, he sat in the refectory pavilion while the monks who had not been invited to dine in their donors' homes finished eating. Then he withdrew to his cell, called "the perfumed chamber," washed his feet, and rested. After the siesta period he came out and preached to the monks who had gathered outside his cell. Then he responded to individual requests for guidance in meditation, after which the monks dispersed to their dwellings. The Buddha took another rest in the late afternoon, then preached to the lay donors and worshippers who came to call on him. Afterward he went to the bathhouse for a cool bath, then paced back and forth in the courtyard or garden and meditated. He concluded the evening (first watch of night) by granting interviews to individual monks. During the second watch of night, he received deities who came for instruction. During the third watch, he rested.

This schedule alternates rest and activity, retirement and sociability, covering a long and busy day at a leisurely pace. It is with good reason that the Vinaya and the elders in charge of the monasteries have consistently emphasized the daily routine and guarded its observance. Buddhism as a way of life is concretely realized in the monastic routine, with its provisions for cultivating morality, wisdom, meditation, and worship; with its scrupulous attention to the correct performance of everyday acts; and with its faith that in the still of the night the gods come down and converse with holy monks in the Saṅgha's moonlit groves.

The Order of Nuns was said to have been instituted reluctantly by the Buddha at the request of his aunt and foster mother Prajāpatī and upon the intercession of Ānanda. The Blessed One conceded that women are able to attain arhant-ship, but laid eight special regulations on the nuns, subordinating them strictly to the Order of Monks. It is perhaps not surprising that an order founded so reluctantly should not have flourished. After the first generation, few distinguished nuns are mentioned.

We have already noted that the first two worshippers of the new Buddha were laymen (p. 22). We have observed (p. 37) that all sects agreed that laymen could attain the first three degrees of sainthood and remain in the household life, while the Sūtras and some Hīnayāna sects affirmed that arhant-ship was open to the layman, though some insisted that immediately after attainment he must either die or become a monk.

The layman in early Buddhism was assigned arduous functions and promised ample rewards in this life and subsequent ones. The monastic orders depended on his donations, and in return they instructed him in Dharma, especially in donation, morality, heaven, the wretchedness of sense-desire, and the benefits of overcoming sense-desire. By keeping the Five Precepts and having profound faith in Buddha, Dharma, and Saṅgha, the layman and laywoman are sure to become "stream-winners," have only happy rebirths, and speedily attain full enlightenment. The virtuous householder is assured increase of wealth because of his zeal, a fine reputation, confidence in public affairs, a calm and unbewildered death, and after death, rebirth in a heaven. Girls are told to become good wives, to be willing and sweet tempered, to honor their husbands' relatives and guests, to be skillful at homecrafts, to manage the servants well, and to protect their husbands' valuables. As a reward, after death they will be born among the Gods of Lovely Form.

The fourfold organization of the Saṅgha results from the segregation of male from female and monastic from lay. Relations between members of the four orders are restricted, so that they will not corrupt one another, and formalized, so that due honor and seniority will be observed. Though the individual layman may well be more moral and more spiritual than any given monk, the former must give precedence to the latter because the yellow-robed orders are superior to the white-clad laity. The nun must look up to the monk, and the laywoman to the layman, because the male sex per se is considered superior to the female, regardless of whether particular women are better than any individual man. The scriptures do not present much of a case for male superiority, and their case for the ceremonial precedence of the monastics is fragmentary and weak. The homeless life is more favorable for attaining sainthood, because it is free from the distractions, temptations, and worries of family life. Hence it is presumed that, in general, monks are more abstemious and zealous than the laity.

The householder is encouraged to take the first five of the ten precepts (*śīla*) undertaken by the novice (see p. 45). *Śīla* is defined as suppressing sins of body and speech in pursuance of a resolution made either in private or before witnesses. The first precept is to refrain from killing living beings. Animals of all sorts are intended, but plants are not. The word is *prāṇin* ("having life breath"). The sin is to know that something is a living being, to intend to kill it, attempt to do so, and to succeed. Unintentional killing is not a sin qua killing, though it may constitute sinful negligence. The layman cannot avoid inadvertently killing small creatures if he practices agriculture, but he is supposed, if he undertakes this precept, to minimize the destruction of small lives.

The second precept is to refrain from taking what has not been given. The sin consists in taking the property of another by force or by stealth. The offense is committed when one knows that the thing belongs to another, and intentionally attempts and successfully executes the act of taking it. If the ownership of an object is unknown, there is an obligation to try to find out whether it is the property of another before taking it.

The third precept is to refrain from misconduct in erotic matters. It concerns intercourse with a forbidden woman (the wife of another, a woman under the care of a guardian, a betrothed woman, a nun, a woman under a vow of chastity), as well as intercourse with one's own wife "by a forbidden passage," in an unsuitable place (that is, a public place or a shrine), at an unsuitable time (that is, when the woman is pregnant, is nursing, or has taken a vow of abstinence). Factors considered here are the rights and obligations of others, the wishes of the woman herself, her health, and that of her child. Notice that the entire discussion pertains to a man's actions. Ancient India commonly assumed that women were by nature wanton, and that consequently the responsibility for keeping them out of trouble lay with their guardians.

The fourth precept is to refrain from lying speech. The sin consists of intentionally concealing the truth, or stating what is known not to be so, in order to deceive another person.

The fifth precept is to refrain from drinking liquor. The reasons given are that liquor does the body little good and much harm, and that by weakening self-control it occasions other sins.

Some Sūtras indicate that the laymen were not usually given instruction on the more technical aspects of wisdom and meditation. Abhidharma and the more abstruse contents of the Sūtras were reserved for monks. One ostensible reason is that the ordinary layman does not have time to understand, let alone practice, such deep and difficult doctrines. But what of the extraordinary householder? Most of the Greek philosophers, the Talmudic sages, the philoso-

phers of classical and imperial China, and the masters of the Hinc
Vaiśeṣika and Mīmāṃsā schools were householders. Probably t
feared that householders would rival them if they became too proficien
deeper Dharma. Such self-interest belies the claim that the monastic orders surpassed the laity in detachment.

We know next to nothing about the life-cycle rites of the Indian Buddhist laity. There were apparently Buddhist funeral and memorial rites, but there is no evidence of a Buddhist wedding ceremony. The Buddhist monk is not a caterer to mundane liturgical needs, like the brāhman. Weddings and other rites of passage may have been purely social ceremonies without participation of religious specialists, or brāhmans may have been employed, or there may have been non-brāhman specialists. In the official Buddhist view, such matters were not religious.

The Rise of Mahāyāna

During the two centuries from 100 B.C. to 100 A.D., there arose within Buddhism a movement that called itself the Mahāyāna, the "Great Course or Vehicle" (*yāna:* "a going, a course, a journey, a vehicle"), in contrast to the Hīnayāna,[1] the "Inferior Vehicle." The Great Course, they said, was that of the bodhisattva, which leads to Buddhahood (supreme, perfect enlightenment), while the Inferior Course leads only to arhant-ship. It appears that the Mahāyāna arose within the Mahāsaṅghika sects, which from the first had disparaged the arhant and had championed doctrines later typical of the Great Course, such as that phenomena are illusory (*māyā*) and empty (*śūnya*), that the true Buddha is transmundane, and that the historical Buddha is a mere apparition of him (see p. 38). The idea of the bodhisattva, the future Buddha, was accepted by all the early sects. The Mahāyāna innovation was to proclaim that the bodhisattva course is open to all, to lay out a path for bodhisattvas to follow, and to create a new pantheon and cult of superhuman bodhisattvas and cosmic Buddhas who respond to the pleas of devotees.

The hallmark of Mahāyāna is its Sūtra literature rather than any one doctrine or practice. All Buddhists accept the authenticity of the Nikāyas or Āgamas. Those who deny that the Mahāyāna Sūtras are the word of the Buddha are Hīnayānists. Those who accept them are Mahāyānists. As there

[1] "Hīnayāna" originated as a Mahāyāna pejorative for those who did not accept the new Sūtras and their doctrines. As the conservatives answered the Mahāyāna propaganda and polemics with silence, they did not adopt any name for themselves *vis-à-vis* Mahāyāna. Consequently modern European, Japanese, and Indian scholars have given them their enemies' name, "Hīnayāna," though without implying any depreciation. Modern Theravādins don't like being called Hīnayānists, but there is no other current term that designates the whole set of sects that arose between the first and the fourth centuries after the Parinirvāṇa. Continued usage will doubtless expunge all derogatory connotations of the term. "Quaker," "Mormon," and even "Christian" started out similarly as labels sarcastically attached by outsiders.

is no special Mahāyāna Vinaya, a monk could accept the new Sūtras without drastic change in his mode of life, and if he happened to be a Mahāsaṅghika, without much alteration in his doctrinal convictions. The very earliest Mahāyāna Sūtras—for example, *The Small Perfection of Wisdom*—do not disparage Hīnayāna, and in fact place the teachings of the bodhisattva course in the mouths of the great arhants. The *Vimalakīrti,* a somewhat later Sūtra, ridicules the arhants and says that even the worst sinner still has a chance to become a Buddha, while the arhant is at a dead end in an inferior nirvāṇa. The still later *Lotus Sūtra* is even more vehemently hostile to Hīnayāna, but adopts a seemingly conciliatory posture, affirming that the arhant is not really condemned to an inferior goal, since there is in reality just one nirvāṇa, that of a Buddha, which even arhants will reach in due course. There could not have been much conflict between the two Courses in 100 B.C. The rift between them widened more and more until in 200 A.D., the *Lotus Sūtra* betrays an irrevocable schism.

The composition of Mahāyāna Sūtras continued from 100 B.C. until 400 A.D., reflecting changes in doctrine and religious life, regional and sectarian differences, and sociocultural factors, some of which can be identified from the evidence of the Sūtras themselves. There are no firsthand historical sources on this literature and the movement which produced it.

In the second century A.D., Mahāyāna authors started publishing *śāstras* ("treatises") in their own names. Although they cited the Sūtras as proofs, and so encouraged the fabrication of new Sūtras to validate new doctrines, they also relied substantially on experience and rational inference. These treatises served to present the Buddhist case to non-Buddhists who rejected the testimony of the Sūtras, and to Hīnayānists who denied the authenticity of the Mahāyāna Sūtras. The new respect for human authors stemmed from a crucial change in Indian elite culture—the emergence of a secular literature (fiction, poetry, and nonfiction), individual authorship, advances in science and knowledge, improvements in techniques of debate and logic, and greater confidence in man's ability to achieve knowledge without the aid of gods or superhuman saints. But the middlebrows and lowbrows continued to crave revelations and stimulate the scripture mills. The Hindus, likewise, went on writing Upaniṣads, Purāṇas, and Āgamas and attributing them to gods and ancient sages. Shortly after the Buddhists stopped faking Sūtras, they started composing Tantras, likewise anonymous and somewhat casually attributed to the Buddha.

There is a Mahāyāna theory of revelation which covertly justifies attribution of these discourses to Śākyamuni. Whatever the enlightened disciples teach is to be considered as the Buddha's own teaching, because they have themselves realized his Dharma and nothing that they teach deviates from it. Early Buddhism, too, had maintained that the words of the arhants agree with those of the Buddha, a confidence somewhat shaken by the frequent falling out of arhants. The Mahāyānists introduced the notion of the Buddha's inspiration or charisma (*adhiṣṭhāna, anubhāva*), through which he infuses thoughts into the minds of men, and sustains the advocates of his Dharma. Since the Mahāyāna Buddha is eternal, omnipresent, and omniscient, it seemed reasonable that his influence would pervade the thoughts of men in the centuries after the Parinirvāṇa, and that their inspirations would have the value of scripture. Early Buddhism had a definite notion of Gautama's charisma (see p. 25), and inasmuch as the Buddha and other arhants can read each other's minds (the third superknowledge, see p. 18), it was not a big step to the idea that the Buddha can implant thoughts in the mind of another. This theory, though, was never openly used to defend the Mahāyāna Sūtras because to do so would have meant giving up the false historical claim the Mahāyānists had foolishly made.

Much obscurity surrounds the origins of Mahāyāna. We do not know where it first arose, but the most likely areas are those where the Mahāsaṅghikas were strong, Andhra and Gandhāra. Scholars who think Iranian and Hellenistic influences played a major part in engendering the Great Vehicle favor North-West India as its birthplace. Considering, though, that bhikṣus wandered the length and breadth of India and stayed freely as guests in the monasteries of all sects, early Mahāyāna ideas doubtless spread rapidly throughout the whole country. The laity, furthermore, were mostly nonsectarian, and as the Great Course developed among them, as well as among the monks, the evolution likely took place in many areas far removed from the spot where it first arose.

Wherever it originated, the Great Vehicle first flourished notably in North-West India, where it exhibited its greatest strength even at 400 A.D., when the Chinese pilgrim Fa-hsien passed through.

The North-West was inhabited by many peoples, Iranian and Greek as well as Indo-Aryan, Zoroastrian and Brāhmanical as well as Buddhist. Buddhism appealed more strongly to non-Indians than did Brāhmanism, though one inscription records the devotion of a Greek to Krishna. Several Hīnayāna sects had achieved missionary successes long before Mahāyāna appeared on the scene. Nevertheless, the contact of peoples and cultures seems to have affected the complexion of Buddhism, to have favored ideas and cults closer to the previous religions of Greece and Persia, and to have loosened the bonds of conservative tradition.

The Teaching of Emptiness

The perfection of wisdom consists in the direct realization that all the dharmas, whether conditioned or unconditioned, are empty. Transmigration is empty, and nirvāṇa is empty; the Buddhas are empty, and the beings whom they guide are empty. Thus there is no essential difference between the relative and the absolute. But what is emptiness, the common predicate of all things? It is absence of own-being (*svabhāva*), a term that means something (1) existing through its own power rather than that of another, (2) possessing an invariant and inalienable mark, and (3) having an immutable essence.

Early Buddhism had ascribed to all conditioned dharmas three universal marks: suffering, impermanence, and no-self. Early Mahāyāna added a fourth, emptiness. But since *ātman* ("self") and *svabhāva* ("own-being") are nearly synonymous, the addition is not really an innovation. Its importance lies more in the value-tone of the word "empty" than in its formal doctrinal content. The early Buddhist emphasis on suffering and impermanence is intended to arouse aversion to worldly life. The Śūnyavādin insistence on emptiness summons the hearer to reevaluate transmigration and achieve release within it rather than fleeing it while still considering it real and important. Intellectually, svabhāvas are false reifications, conceptual figments. Emotionally, they are the foci of obsessions, the illusory idols which enslave the passions. The contemplation of emptiness is an intellectual and emotional therapy. The aim is not to deny commonsense reality to things as experienced in the commonsense world, but to cleanse one's vision of false views, and so to see the world "as it really is," that is, to see its "suchness" (*tathatā*).

Empty entities are neither existent nor inexistent. Either extreme would be heretical, in Śūnyavāda as in Early Buddhism (see p. 30). So emptiness is not an absolute substance, not a stuff out of which all things are made, like the Upaniṣadic brahman. Rather, it is the fact that no immutable substance exists and none underlies phenomena. But emptiness is equivalent to dependent coarising, the principle which Gautama enunciated as the Middle Way between being and nonbeing (see p. 30).

Dependent coarising, though, is a descriptive law rather than a substantial entity. Ancient India was especially puzzled over the ontological status of abstractions, descriptions, and relational laws. Realists kept trying to reduce them to things, whereas the Buddhists consistently analyzed things into relations and principles. One of the chief obstacles for modern people trying to understand śūnyatā is that science discarded the substance-and-attribute mode of explanation centuries ago; and, thanks to popular science, we are all Śūnyavādins nowadays in our serious metaphysics, while often remaining naïve svabhāva-vādins in our theology and self-image. On the one hand, emptiness seems too obvious to be intellectually significant. On the other, it gives offense by attacking the emotional props that uphold the ordinary, unenlightened personality.

Throughout the ages people, alarmed and repelled by the idea of emptiness, have equated it with nothingness, an error against which the Sūtras and treatises warn repeatedly. Emptiness is the expeller of wrong views, but emptiness wrongly apprehended is as dangerous as a snake wrongly grasped or a spell wrongly recited. It is as wrong to crave obliteration into nothingness as to cling to transmigration and long for eternal existence.

The teaching of emptiness repudiates dualities: between the conditioned and the unconditioned, between subject and object, between the pure and the impure, between the relative and the absolute. It cannot be called monism, however, because it denies that reality is either a plurality or a unity; it is simply beyond individuation and numbers, both of which are fictive concepts and mere designations. What, then, is reality? It is called the Dharma-realm. Dharma-nature, the Dharma-body (*dharmakāya*), the acme of the real, suchness (*tathatā*), and the highest entity or absolute (*paramārtha*). But it is *saṃsāra* ("transmigration") seen as it really is by the vision of the saints—nondifferent from nirvāṇa.

This doctrine comes to terms with the early Buddhist quandary about the relationship between the nirvāṇa-realm and the world. Not only is nirvāṇa immanent in the world, but neither exists apart from the other. The world is a phantom conjured up by karmic action, the magician. But the phantom-maker is himself a phantom (*māyā*). These phantoms exist inasmuch as they appear and act, but inexist insofar as they are insubstantial and impermanent. To cause and reside in such a phantom world does not degrade nirvāṇa to the level of a commonsense thing, nor does it hypostasize it as a separate absolute.

Nirvāṇa is by definition changeless, while dependent coarising is the process of change. Śūnyavādins say, though, that dependent coarising is noncinematic. When seen from the absolute standpoint, past, present, and future are all observed simultaneously, like a painting, while from the conventional standpoint they appear as a series, like a movie. The contrast between the two truths (conventional and absolute) is the basic principle of the *Prajñā-pāramitā Sūtras,* and all their apparent paradoxes merely insist that what is true from one standpoint is false from the other. This epistemological dualism is the price that Śūnyavāda pays for ontological nondualism.

Emptiness has far-reaching consequences for the religious life. Monks in training who are ridden with feelings of guilt and shame because they have infringed the Vinaya are told to appease their guilt by meditation on its emptiness. This does not give them license to sin, but it liberates them from the burden of evil. The bodhisattva can work and play in the secular world without fear of contamination from sense objects, because he knows that intrinsically they are neither pure nor impure. He associates with merchants, kings, harlots, and drunkards without falling into avarice, arrogance, lust, or dissipation. He accepts and excels in the arts and sciences, welcoming them as good means to benefit and edify living beings. He recognizes the religious capacities of women, listening respectfully when they preach the Dharma, because he knows that maleness and femaleness are both empty. A rich man can be a good bodhisattva if, realizing that his wealth is empty, he is humble and generous. A poor man, too, can excel in holiness if he recognizes that his poverty is empty, and doesn't let it impair his self-respect. It is all right to be a monk, but a layman often has better opportunities to practice skill in good means, if he remembers that everything is empty.

The Śūnyavādin Sūtras assert and illustrate but do not prove their theses.

They employ much persuasive rhetoric and very little inference and formal argument. Nāgārjuna (*c.* 150–250 A.D.) grieved that the Hindu philosophical schools, employing the Nyāya methods of argumentation, were outclassing the Buddhists in the fashionable interschool debates, so he set out to argue the Śūnyavādin case against both Hīnayānists and non-Buddhists using the standard rules of debate and certain special forms of argument. He took his main concepts and definitions from the Sūtras, but he tried to refute his opponents on their own grounds rather than on the authority of scriptures that they did not accept.

Nāgārjuna is the founder of the Mādhyamika or Madhyamaka school, so-called because it claims to maintain the Middle Path (*Madhyamā Pratipad*) between being and nonbeing which the Buddha declared in his sermon to Kaccāna (see p. 30). He wrote two didactic works preaching morality and the way to nirvāṇa in straightforward, conventional, and positive language. He is also the reputed author of several Mahāyāna hymns. But his best-known work is the *Middle Stanzas* (*Madhyamaka-kārikās*), a polemical treatise of about 450 verses in which he refutes a wide range of "wrong views."

Nāgārjuna's immediate disciple Āryadeva carried on the polemic tradition, but he was inferior to his master in style and intelligence. Mādhyamika became quite popular, but did not make qualitative advances until about 500 A.D., when Bhāvaviveka adopted the epistemology and logic of the logician Dignāga, and tackled a host of problems that his school had previously ignored. Candrakīrti then attacked Bhāvaviveka, severely criticizing his use of logic, and going back to the position of the earlier Mādhyamika commentators. Bhāvaviveka wrote one of the first handbooks of the Indian philosophical systems, and Candrakīrti composed an excellent compendium of the bodhisattva path, the *Introduction to Madhyamaka*. Both authors display a superb style and rigorous thought.

The Bodhisattva Path

Mahāyāna is synonymous with the course (*yāna*) or career (*caryā*) of the bodhisattva. In the early Mahāyāna Sūtras (composed before the second century A.D.), this is a simple path beginning with arousing the thought (that is, aspiration) for supreme, perfect enlightenment, and practicing the six perfections (*pāramitā*) until the goal is reached. Between 100 and 300 A.D., the doctrine of the ten bodhisattva stages (*bhūmi*) was introduced, and an elaborate schema of paths and stages was devised.

The Mahāyāna Sūtras address their teaching equally to the monastics and laity, exhorting both to recite, copy, and explain the Sūtras, an enterprise which monachizing Hīnayāna sects reserved for the monks and nuns. But though the laity and monastics were regarded as equal in some respects, it was still maintained that the monastic orders were superior, and the layman still had to pay formal honor to the monk. Only some Sūtras, the libertarian ones, authorize the layman to preach Dharma to monks. The most famous of such Sūtras, the *Vimalakīrti,* shows the householder bodhisattva encouraging a crowd of young patricians to leave the household life. When they protest that they cannot do so without their parents' permission, Vimalakīrti tells them to arouse the thought of enlightenment and practice diligently, since that is equivalent to "going forth." Far from diminishing the monastic vocation, this concession is a second-best for those unable to take the yellow robe.

Nothing like European anticlericalism is found in the Sūtras of the Great Vehicle. There is one lurid description of corruption in the monasteries, of wicked monks who, "destitute of shame and morality, impudent as crows, arrogant, ill-tempered, consumed by jealousy, conceit, and presumption," engaged in commerce and litigation and cohabited with women. Evidently some monasteries fell into the hands of opportunists who disregarded the Vinaya while enjoying use of the Saṅgha's property and privileges.

Though the literature reveals a number of upāsaka preachers, it mentions no legitimate noncelibate communal life, and no householder clergy. The householder bodhisattva was welcome to study meditation and philosophy, and probably was allowed to spend protracted periods of retreat in the monasteries. He could teach the doctrine, and was encouraged to propagate it. But, so far as we know, the Mahāyāna Sūtras were composed by monks, and there is not a single important treatise attributed to any Indian Buddhist layman.

The bodhisattva saṅgha was evidently a fraternity within the general Buddhist Community. It had no special monastic rule, and its householder sections were probably loose-knit associations like those that gather around modern Hindu holy men and temples. There was an ordination rite for the upāsaka bodhisattva, modeled on the bhikṣu's ceremony rather than on the less solemn Hīnayāna upāsaka initiation.

The way begins with the teaching of a Buddha, a bodhisattva, or some other spiritual friend. Seeds of virtue are planted in the mind of the hearer, and from much hearing he comes to perform good deeds, through which he acquires more and more roots of goodness. After many lives, thanks to the infused grace of the various teacher-saviors and the merit earned by responding to them, a person becomes able to put forth the thought of enlightenment. The two motives for this aspiration are one's own desire for bodhi, and compassion for all living beings who suffer in saṃsāra. Initially the motivation is both egotistic and altruistic, but along the path one realizes the sameness of self and others, and transcends the duality of purpose. Arousing the thought of bodhi is an extremely meritorious deed. It cancels past bad karma, increases merit, wards off bad rebirths, and assures good ones. In these respects, it corresponds to "winning the stream" in Early Buddhism, since the stream-winner, too, will never be reborn in the woeful destinies and is confirmed in the course to enlightenment (see p. 27). "Arousing the thought" is a decisive conversion experience with profound psychological effects. It is compared to a pearl, to the ocean, to sweet music, to a shade-giving tree, to a convenient bridge, to soothing moonbeams, to the sun's rays, to a universal panacea, and to an infallible elixir.

The new bodhisattva proceeds to consolidate his bodhicitta and advance on the path by cultivating good qualities and working for the welfare of living beings. He makes a set of vows or earnest resolutions. Some vows are quite general, for instance: "When we have crossed the stream, may we ferry others across. When we are liberated, may we liberate others." Some bodhisattvas' vows are very specific and pragmatic, for example those of Dharmākara, who later became the Buddha Amitābha. He made three or four dozen vows, in the form "May I not attain supreme, perfect enlightenment until such-and-such a benefit is assured beings who are born in my Buddha-country." Taking the precepts is an Early Buddhist forerunner of Mahāyāna vow-making in that it is a formal act of commitment and involves a greater forfeiture of merit if one transgresses than if one had not made a vow. Bodhisattva vows are usually binding until the end of the bodhisattva career, a matter of eons. Even when the great bodhisattva has passed beyond dualistic cognitions and intentions, he is motivated, as if on automatic pilot, by the force of his original vows.

The bodhisattva is supposed to declare his vows in the presence of a Buddha, which means that he must wait until a Buddha appears in the world. The Tathāgata then gives the bodhisattva a prediction (see pp. 27–28) that after *x* number of ages he will become a Buddha of such-and-such a name, reigning in such-and-such a Buddha-country, which will have such-and-such excellences. Ordinary bodhisattvas who have not yet had the good fortune to be born in the same generation as a Buddha make their vows in the presence of other human bodhisattvas, or even with the Buddhas and bodhisattvas of the ten directions as their witnesses.

The six perfections are the main course of the bodhisattva career. As we have noted (p. 39), these virtues are all advocated in the Early Buddhist Canon, and extreme instances of them are extolled in the Jātakas. Mahāyāna differs from Hīnayāna in making the extremes the model for ordinary devotees.

A virtue is practiced to perfection when the most difficult acts are executed with a mind free from discriminatory ideas, without self-consciousness, ulterior motives, or self-congratulation. The perfect giver, for example, doesn't think "I give," and has no fictive concepts about the gift, the recipient, or the reward that ensues from the act. Thus the perfection of wisdom (*prajñā-pāramitā*) is necessary in order to attain the other five perfections.

The perfection of donation (*dāna*) consists of giving material things, Dharma-instructions and one's own body and life to all beings, then in turn transferring or reassigning the ensuing merit to supreme enlightenment and the welfare of other beings, rather than allowing it to earn one future bliss in the world. The bodhisattva practices dāna, and instigates others to do likewise.

The perfection of morality (*śīla*) consists of following the ten good paths of action, transferring the merit, and instigating others to do likewise. The ten are: not killing, stealing, or fornicating; not lying, slandering, speaking harshly, or chattering frivolously; and not having covetous thoughts, hostile thoughts, or false views.

The perfection of patience (*kṣānti*) is founded in nonanger and nonagitation. It means patient endurance of hardship and pain, forbearance and forgiveness toward those who injure and abuse the bodhisattva, and patient assent to difficult and uncongenial doctrines.

The perfection of vigor (*vīrya*) means unremitting energy and zeal in overcoming one's faults and cultivating virtues, in studying Dharma and the arts and sciences, and in doing good works for the welfare of others. Vīrya is derived from *vīra* ("a martial man, a hero"). It corresponds to right effort, the sixth member of the Holy Eightfold Path of Early Buddhism, but more explicitly signifies heroic endeavor to benefit other living beings.

The perfection of meditation (*dhyāna*) consists of entering all the meditative trances, concentrations, and attainments, yet not accepting rebirth in the paradises to which such states normally destine one in the next life.

The perfection of wisdom (*prajñā-pāramitā*) is personified as a goddess, because *prajñā* is grammatically feminine. She is the mother of all the Buddhas, since through her they become enlightened ones. A famous hymn endows her with feminine traits and maternal loving-kindness.

The *Prajñā-pāramitā Sūtras* say over and over again that the doctrine that things neither arise nor cease is supremely difficult, that it causes fear and aversion in the tender-minded, and that the bodhisattva who can accept it is a great hero (*mahāsattva*). Three degrees of assent (*kṣānti*) are distinguished. The first is acceptance of the words of the teaching. The second is conforming assent, attained in the sixth bodhisattva-bhūmi, and consisting of an intense but not definitive conviction. The third is patient acceptance that the dharmas are nonarising. It is said by later texts to be attained in the eighth bhūmi, and it is concomitant with reaching the nonrelapsing state. We have seen that the nonreturner is the second highest level of holy person in Early Buddhism, and that the stream-winner is assured of not falling back into the states of woe (see p. 27). The Mahāyāna concept of nonrelapsing is a reworking of the old ideas.

The early bhūmi theory seems to have recognized just seven bodhisattva stages, with acceptance that the dharmas are nonarising and that the nonrelapsing states occurring in the seventh bhūmi. The number of bhūmis was increased from seven to ten about 200 A.D. Variant lists of stations and stages circulated for a while, but eventually the following became standard:

(a) The stage of the "lineage," where the beginner strives to acquire a stock of merit and knowledge. It extends from the first thought of enlightenment until the "experience of heat," the first signpost of success in meditation.

(b) The stage of "practicing with conviction." Here the bodhisattva cultivates four "factors of penetration," namely "meditative heat," "climax," "patience," and "highest mundane dharma." These meditative experiences overcome and expel the antithesis between subject and object, and lead to nondiscriminative knowledge.

(c) The ten bodhisattva stages, namely: (1) the joyful, (2) the stainless, (3) the illumining, (4) the flaming, (5) the very-hard-to-conquer (6) the face-to-face, (7) the far-going, (8) the immovable, (9) good-insight, and (10) Dharma-cloud. In each successive stage, one of the pāramitās is supposed to be practiced concertedly. Four pāramitās were added to the early list of six for the sake of symmetry: (7) skill in means, (8) vows, (9) power, and (10) knowledge. The first bodhisattva-bhūmi corresponds to the path of vision, which follows immediately after "highest mundane dharma," and is characterized by nondual awareness.

(d) The Buddha-stage follows the diamond-like samādhi which is the last event on the "path of cultivation." This concentration plays an important role in Abhidharma, too, where it is realized by the bodhisattva as he sits on the Diamond Throne (see pp. 1, 17), and in it he fulfils the perfections of dhyāna and prajñā in the moment just before he attains bodhi. It is this samādhi which destroys all the residues of defilement. Mahāyāna doctrine maintains that the terminal path consists in awareness that the causes of suffering have been destroyed and will never arise again. In other words, the bodhisattva's final realization is identical with the arhant's (see p. 18).

There were some differences of opinion about the duration of the bodhisattva career, but the prevalent view was that it takes three immeasurable kalpas: one to or through the first bodhisattva-bhūmi, one from there through the seventh bhūmi, and one for bhūmis eight to ten.

The Celestial Bodhisattvas

The chief innovation in the Mahāyāna pantheon is the class of great bodhisattvas, also called mahāsattvas ("great beings"). The *Lotus Sūtra* mentions by name twenty-three; the *Vimalakīrti* names fifty-some. Of these, the most important are Mañjuśrī, Avalokiteśvara, Mahāsthāmaprāpta, and Maitreya. All four figure as interlocutors in Mahāyāna Sūtras, where they appear as men and converse with the great disciples and Śākyamuni. These great beings are nonhistorical in that there is no evidence that any one of them is an apotheosis of a human hero, as Rāma certainly was and Krishna probably was. Strangely, no Sūtra preaches devotion to a celestial bodhisattva until the third century A.D., a full three centuries after these beings entered the literature. The strategic function of these bodhisattvas in the Sūtras is to serve as Mahāyāna counterparts to the great arhants in the Nikāyas. The nonrelapsing bodhisattva stage is so exalted that no actual persons could be found to represent it.

Maitreya is the earliest cult bodhisattva. A Pali Sūtra predicts that in the distant future there will arise in the world a Blessed One named Metteya

(Pali for Maitreya), who will have thousands of disciples just as Śākyamuni has hundreds. Another Pali Sūtra lists, with particulars, six Buddhas of the past whom Gautama remembers through his own paranormal powers, as well as through revelation from the gods. Stūpas of the former Buddhas were built as early as the third century B.C.; but if the extinct Buddhas were worthy of reverence, how much more so the coming one, now a bodhisattva residing in the Tuṣita heaven (see p. 24) and awaiting his last birth? The pious might look forward to the utopia, and to pass the interlude happily and be sure of rebirth along with Maitreya when he comes, they could seek rebirth in the Tuṣita paradise. An efficacious means to secure a desired rebirth is to concentrate one's thoughts on it at the moment of death. Thus King Duṭṭhagāmaṇi of Ceylon, dying in 80 B.C., fixed his last thoughts on Maitreya's paradise where, the chronicles assure us, he was reborn.

While Mahāyāna affirmed that saṃsāra is suffering and that one should try to get out of it, and while it assured eventual nirvāṇa to all or most adherents, its willingness to postpone attainment for vast ages betrays an accommodation to saṃsāra that was foreign to the early teaching. Like the youthful Augustine, who prayed "Lord, give me chastity, but not yet," the bodhisattvas were quite content to wait. This attitude also appears in the Theravāda tradition. On his deathbed the Elder Saṅgharakkhita disclosed that contrary to popular belief he was not an arhant: "Thinking to see the Blessed One Metteya, I did not try for insight." But so as not to disappoint the crowds who had gathered, he made an effort and immediately became an arhant.

All Hīnayāna sects acknowledged Maitreya, and the Theravāda tradition recognizes no other bodhisattva in the present age. He was conceived as a historical bodhisattva, and where the Canon had nothing to say, extra-canonical tradition invented history.

Maitreya, unlike the Buddhas before him, is alive, so he can respond to the prayers of worshippers. Being compassionate, as his name indicates, he willingly grants help, and being a high god in his present birth, he has the power to do so. His cult thus offers its devotees the advantages of theism and Buddhism combined. India was caught up in the surge of messianic expectations which, originating probably in Iran, coursed through the Mediterranean world after 200 B.C.

Buddhism was more hospitable than Hinduism to the messianic idea because it was more open to Western influences, and because from the first it took history and pseudohistory more seriously. Accustomed to thinking of the past in terms of teacher-pupil lineages, Buddhists came in due course to anticipate the future sage, just as the Hebrews came to dream of a future anointed prophet-king after musing long on the series of prophets and kings in their ancient history. Each Messiah, though, accrued collateral attributes and functions. Christ assimilated the figures of the suffering servant, the Son of God, and the dying God, to the nuclear concept of the coming king and judge. Maitreya proved no less accommodating. He became a god of light, like

Ahura Mazda, Jehovah, Christ, Krishna, and all the Buddhas and other bodhisattvas. This was probably not due to Iranian influences (Persia is not the only place where the sun shines), but it undoubtedly made the cult more congenial to worshippers of the sacred fire, of Ahura Mazda and Mithra. As a figure of light and of the future, Maitreya came to be the inspirer, a role he shares with Mañjuśrī and with Brahmā.

Just as the Buddha had received revelations and inspirations from the devas, Mahāyāna masters went into trance and journeyed to the Tuṣita heaven, where Maitreya revealed Dharma-themes to them. On occasion, too, he descended to earth to divulge texts, which makes it exceedingly difficult to decide whether the Yogācārin texts attributed to "Lord Maitreya" are or are not the works of some human author who took that name. As the "Friendly One," Maitreya became the consoler of Dharma-masters and seekers when they were afflicted with doubt and discouragement. In his capacity as the Friend, he also receives confessions of sins, and guides the departed after death, an office the Bodhisattva Avalokiteśvara and the Buddha Amitābha also perform. If the devout are bound for Maitreya's paradise when they die, what more natural than that he should come and welcome them?

Maitreya is, along with the future Śākyamuni, the bodhisattva most often represented in the Greco-Buddhist sculpture of Gandhāra. He is shown standing, squatting, or sitting European style on a chair, wearing a topknot bound with a fillet, and carrying a Brāhman's water jar. In Central Asia, numerous statues, paintings, and texts discovered by archaeologists testify to his immense popularity. He was adopted by the Manicheans, who fused Mithras Invictus, Jesus Christ, and Ajita Maitreya into one composite savior figure.

Mañjuśrī shares with Maitreya preeminence among the bodhisattvas in Mahāyāna Sūtras up to 300 A.D. In the *Lotus Sūtra* he remembers deeds of former Buddhas which were unknown even to Maitreya. In the *Vimalakīrti,* he alone of all Śākyamuni's disciples has wisdom and eloquence enough to stand up to that formidable householder Vimalakīrti. In the *Gaṇḍavyūha,* he counsels the youth Sudhana in his search for enlightenment. Many smaller Sūtras are devoted to his legend, his attributes, and his teachings. Curiously, he is scarcely mentioned in the *Prajñā-pāramitā Sūtras*. And he is absent from the Buddhist art of all schools—Gandhāra, Mathurā, Amarāvatī, Nāgārjunakoṇḍa—prior to 400 A.D. When he does appear in art, he is shown as a bodhisattva bhikṣu, with a five-pointed coiffure or tiara, a sword (to cut ignorance) in his right hand, a book (the Prajñā-pāramitā) in his left, and a lion for his mount.

The name Mañjuśrī means "gentle or sweet glory." He is also called *Mañjughoṣa* ("Sweet Voice") and *Vāgīśvara* ("Lord of Speech"). This last epithet also belongs to Brahmā, whose roles as patron of science, custodian of memory, lord of inspiration, and most ancient of beings Mañjuśrī takes over in the Mahāyāna pantheon. The nucleus around which this bodhisattva-figure grew is a Gandharva named *Pañcaśikha* ("Five-Crest"), who appears in wonder-tales in the Pali Sūtras. In one tale, Śakra and the Gods of the Thirty-Three are assembled in their annual convention. A radiant splendor announces the imminent manifestation of Brahmā Sanaṃkumāra ("Forever-a-youth"). This great god's proper form is too subtle to be visible to the Gods of the Thirty-Three, so he creates an apparition-body "in appearance like the youth Five-Crest." Just as a golden image outshines humans, so Brahmā's apparition outshines the other gods in color and in glory. His voice is fluent, intelligible, sweet, audible, continuous, distinct, deep, and resonant. In this guise, Brahmā proceeds to preach the Dharma to Indra and his hosts.

Mañjuśrī's standard epithet is *kumāra-bhūta,* "in the form of a youth," or "having become the crown prince." The former meaning is the earlier, and applies equally to the Gandharva, who like all angels never grows old, and to Brahmā, whose epithet is "Forever-a-youth." Mañjuśrī is the crown prince of Dharma because, like other tenth-stage bodhisattvas, he will next become a King of Dharma, a Buddha.

In due course, devotees endowed Mañjuśrī with a history invented out of whole cloth. Seventy myriads of kalpas ago and seventy-two hundred billion Buddha-fields to the East of this world, Mañjuśrī was a pious king who offered worship to a Tathāgata, and aroused the thought of bodhi. He resolved to pursue an endless career to the end of transmigration, and not to hurry to enlightenment but to stay in saṃsāra as long as there remained even one being to be saved. Though he has now fulfilled all the virtues of a Buddha, he has never considered becoming one. But eventually he will become a Tathāgata. This implies that there will come a time when the last living being has been saved, a rare eschatological statement in the Buddhist tradition.

The doctrinaire thesis that all bodhisattvas take three immeasurable kalpas to reach their final goal is contradicted by the *Larger Prajñā-pāramitā Sūtra.* It says that some bodhisattvas obtain supreme perfect enlightenment as soon as they arouse the thought of bodhi, while others, animated by great love and compassion, devote the longest possible time to the welfare of all living beings. Mañjuśrī took as long as possible to reach the tenth stage, and will stay there until universal salvation is reached.

Tenth-stage bodhisattvas have the ability to manifest themselves anywhere in any condition. They enter the Hero's-journey Concentration, manifesting themselves in all parts of the universe as bodhisattvas at various stages, as residents of the paradises, and as Buddhas. They go through the standard episodes of a Buddha's career and enter parinirvāṇa, but do not in fact become extinct. The Sūtras mention Mañjuśrī as residing in diverse Buddha-fields in the present and in the past, and as being a Buddha in other world-realms now, as well as ages ago.

Mañjuśrī usually appears to human beings in dreams. The chronicles record that a dozen or more great masters "saw the face of Mañjuśrī." Anyone who merely hears Mañjuśrī's name uttered subtracts many kalpas from his time in transmigration. Whoever worships him is born time and again in the

Buddha-family and is protected by Mañjuśrī's power. Those who meditate on Mañjuśrī's statue and his teaching will be similarly fortunate and will reach enlightenment. If a devotee recites the *Śūraṃgama-samādhi Sūtra* and chants Mañjuśrī's name, then within seven days Mañjuśrī will come to him, appearing in a dream if bad karma hinders the supplicant from receiving direct vision. Mañjuśrī also takes on the form of a poor man or an orphan and appears to those who are devoted to him. The wise man should contemplate Mañjuśrī's superhuman physical marks. If he does so, he will soon see the Bodhisattva.

Avalokiteśvara (Ch. Kuan-yin) first appears as a mere name in the lists at the beginning of the *Vimalakīrti* and later, the *Lotus Sūtra.* His first significant role is in the *Sukhāvati-vyūha Sūtra,* where he and Mahāsthāmaprāpta are Amitābha Buddha's chief attendants. They are the only Bodhisattvas in Sukhāvatī whose light is boundless, and, owing to them, that world-realm is luminous always and everywhere. The two of them used to be men in this Sahā-world, and upon dying went to Sukhāvatī.

The *Avalokiteśvara Sūtra* was incorporated into the *Lotus Sūtra* as late as the third century A.D. To this day, though, it circulates as an independent work in China and Japan, where it is the main item in the liturgy of the Kuan-yin cult. A few verses at the end describe Sukhāvatī, and say that Avalokiteśvara stands now to the left of Amitābha and fans him. The rest of the text says nothing about Amitābha, and shows Avalokiteśvara as an omnipresent, omnipotent savior-deity subordinate to no one. He has purified his vows for countless kalpas under millions of Buddhas. He possesses all virtues, and is especially rich in love and compassion. His "skill in means" is infinite, and through it he takes whatever form will help living beings. He adopts the guise of a Buddha, a bodhisattva, a disciple, Brahmā, Indra, and other gods. Like Mañjuśrī, he has played the role of a Buddha and will play it again, without getting trapped in extinction. In this respect the celestial bodhisattvas are superior to the Buddhas.

Avalokiteśvara grants multifarious boons to those who remember him and recite his name. The merit from adoring him is equal to that from worshipping and serving an incredible number of Buddhas. Those who adore him are saved from lust, hostility, and folly. A woman who worships him will get a son or daughter, whichever she wishes. Anyone in distress will be freed from danger and anxiety. For example, if you fall into a fire, think of Avalokiteśvara and it will be quenched. Similarly he rescues those who invoke him from shipwreck, falling off a mountain, missiles, armed robbers and enemies, execution, chains and shackles, witchcraft, demons, wild beasts, snakes, and thunderbolts.

This Bodhisattva is usually represented in art as a bejewelled layman wearing a high crown with a cross-legged image of Amitābha in the front of it. He often holds a lotus in his hand. In the Vajrayāna period (600–1200 A.D.) he came to be represented with eleven heads, or with four, ten, twelve, twenty-four, or a thousand arms. In China he was even metamorphosed into a female.

Mahāsthāmaprāpta is mentioned in the lists at the beginning of the *Lotus Sūtra* and the *Vimalakīrti*. Śākyamuni addresses a discourse to him in Chapter 19 of the *Lotus*, and as already noted, the *Sukhāvatī-vyūha Sūtra* places him on a par with Avalokiteśvara as an attendant of Amitābha's. In Far Eastern art he is frequently represented standing on the right of Amitābha while Avalokiteśvara stands on the left.

Samantabhadra ("Universal Sage") became popular rather late. He is not mentioned at the beginning of the *Lotus Sūtra*, but in Chapter 26, a late addition, he comes with a fabulous retinue to the Sahā-world to ask Śākyamuni to expound the *Lotus Sūtra*. He promises to protect the monks who keep this Sūtra, to avert the menaces of human enemies and demons. Mounted on a white elephant with six tusks, he will accompany the preacher, and will appear and remind him when he forgets part of the text. If the devotee walks around for twenty-one days, then Samantabhadra will show his body on the twenty-first, will stimulate the devotee, and will give him talismanic spells.

The Celestial Buddhas

We have seen (p. 38) how the Mahāsaṅghikas maintained that the Buddha is supermundane and yet forever active in the world, infinite and eternal, transcendental and immanent. Since Dharma is all these things, it stands to reason that his *Dharmakāya* ("Dharma-body") should be likewise. The early sects all wrestled with the apparent anomaly that the Buddha, though extremely wise, powerful, and good, lived a mere eighty years and then ceased to function in saṃsāra. If he could have lived for a kalpa, why didn't he do so? (p. 35). Over the centuries, the steady pressure of wishful thinking produced an answer: Gautama didn't really enter extinction; he only seemed to do so. His form-body was just an apparition (*nirmāna, nirmita*), a conjurer's illusion (*māyā*). Though Buddhism denied that there is a personal Creator, it assigned the same functions to Dharma (= dependent coarising), and by emphasizing the fictive, insubstantial, and transient character of phenomena, came to view the conditioned world as a figment of cosmic imagination. So when the historical Buddha was considered an apparition, he was not held to be less real than anything else in the world.

Once granted that the historic Gautama was an apparition of the everlasting Dharmakāya, it seemed reasonable that there should be apparition-bodies in all times and places, that benevolent omnipotence should respond to the needs of all suffering beings. There must be Buddhas elsewhere in the universe, as well as in the past and future of this Sahā-world-realm.

Early Buddhist cosmology had posited just one world system (*loka-dhātu*) consisting of four continents on earth, and assorted hells below and heavens above. Later it came to be held that the immediate universe, "the three-thousand great-thousand world-realm" consists of 1000^3 such worlds. In the ten directions (East, Southeast, South, Southwest, West, Northwest, North, Northeast, Nadir, and Zenith), there are universes "as numerous as the sands of the Ganges." Some but not all of these universes are Buddha-fields, where a Tathāgata lives and teaches the Dharma.

The Mahāsaṅghikas very early asserted that there are Buddhas in all directions and in all the universes. What the Mahāyāna did was to produce names for such Buddhas and their countries, legends about their origins, and vivid circumstantial descriptions of the scenery and spiritual amenities of certain Buddha-lands. Gautama's career is the paradigm for all these other Buddhas' legends, and the celestial Buddha-lands are Never-Never Lands fashioned after terrestial models. These tales undoubtedly have an experiential basis in the visions of Buddhas, bodhisattvas, and paradises that resulted from the meditation on the Buddha and the gods that are recommended even in Theravāda works. We have seen already that much of Mahāyāna meditation seeks to obtain the appearance of bodhisattvas in dreams or in transic visions. Manifestations of Buddhas and Buddha-lands were sought and obtained by the same means. In addition, it was believed that Gautama and his great bodhisattvas could reveal other Buddha-lands through their superknowledges and supervening powers, so that ordinary people could see them directly.

This Mahāyāna space fiction expresses a radical expansion of world view and a corresponding change in values. The drama of salvation was no longer confined to this Sahā-world-realm, and help from outside might be expected. Sākyamuni's followers were not spiritual orphans, because extraterrestrial friends stood always ready to protect them—not only gods like Śakra, Brahmā, and the Four Great Kings, but great bodhisattvas and Buddhas also. This feeling of endless space populated by spiritual beings is perhaps the nuclear world view of classical Indian civilization.

Śākyamuni remained the foremost of the celestial Buddhas until Tantrism transformed the Indian Buddhist pantheon. The *Lotus* ranks among the greatest of the Mahāyāna Sūtras not because of profound technical philosophy, of which it contains only a few fragments, but because it teaches artfully, in graphic parables and concrete religious language, that the historical Gautama is in reality an everlasting, everpresent cosmic father.

In the *Lotus Sūtra,* the Buddha Śākyamuni tells Śāriputra that only a Tathāgata knows all the dharmas as they really are. As the Dharma is exceedingly difficult, the Buddhas employ their supreme skill in good means to accommodate the doctrine to living beings' varying capacities. Śāriputra pleads with the Buddha to reveal the true Dharma. The Buddha consents, and declares: "It is for a sole aim that the Tathāgata appears in the world, namely to impart to living beings the knowledge and vision of a Tathāgata." The Buddhas, furthermore, preach the Dharma by means of just One Vehicle, the Buddha-yāna. But when a Buddha appears in a degenerate epoch, among beings who are corrupt and lacking in merit, he uses the expedient device of the Three Vehicles (arhant, private-buddha, and bodhisattva). Śāriputra rejoices to hear the Buddha say that the arhants are not condemned to an inferior nirvāṇa, that they too will reach supreme, perfect enlightenment. Śākyamuni then predicts that Śāriputra will become a Buddha in the distant future.

Śāriputra asks the Buddha to dispel the perplexity that the idea of the One Vehicle has occasioned among sincere Hīnayānists in the assembly. Gautama then tells the parable of the burning house. A rich householder had a vast and decrepit mansion inhabited by hundreds of living beings. A fire broke out, and the man devised a stratagem to get his twenty young sons out of the house. They didn't come when he called them, because they were too busy playing to notice the flames. So he told them that toy carts—bullock carts, goat carts, and deer carts—awaited them outside. The boys came out, and found that there was only one kind of cart, a magnificent bullock cart.

Śāriputra agrees that the father was not guilty of falsehood, as his story of the three carts was an expedient to save his children. Śākyamuni says that the Buddha, being the father of the world, is not guilty of falsehood, either, when as an upāya he announces that there are three vehicles. Just as the rich man gave each of his sons the best of carts, even so the Buddha leads all beings to the same supreme enlightenment.

The Buddha tells a parable. A rain cloud comes up and pours water equally upon all kinds of grass, shrubs, and trees. Rooted in the same soil and vivified by the same water, they nonetheless grow to different height according to their natures. Likewise, the Dharma of the Tathāgata is of one essence, yet each responds according to his capacity. The bodhisattvas are the trees, while the Hīnayānists (men of the Two Vehicles) are the lesser plants.

A giant stūpa arises in the sky, and hovers there resplendent with jewels and ornaments. A voice from it praises Śākyamuni for proclaiming well the *Lotus Sūtra*. When the multitude is gathered, Śākyamuni opens the stūpa, and there is revealed the body of the "extinct" Buddha Prabhūtaratna sitting crosslegged as if in samādhi. He repeats his praise of Śākyamuni, to the astonishment of the assembly who think Prabhūtaratna has been extinct for many eons. Prabhūtaratna moves over, and Śākyamuni sits beside him.

The point of this episode is that a Tathāgata who enters parinirvāṇa may not actually be extinct; he may only seem so. Likewise, what seems like a live Buddha may be an apparition magically created by Śākyamuni.

Śākyamuni states, "Many trillions of kalpas ago I realized supreme perfect enlightenment." When the Tathāgata who so long ago reached perfect enlightenment goes through a semblance of attainment, he does so in order to lead beings to maturity. Without becoming extinct, he makes a show of extinction, so that weak beings will not take his continuing presence for granted. When these people are convinced that the apparition of Tathāgatas is rare, they become more zealous.

Śākyamuni declares that he resides forever on Mount Gṛdhrakūṭa preaching the Dharma. When the unenlightened imagine that this world is engulfed in flames at the end of a kalpa, it is really a paradise with gardens, palaces, and aerial cars, teeming with gods and men.

The idea that this wretched world is really a splendid, pure Buddha-field occurs also in the *Vimalakīrti.* This idea has also enjoyed considerable currency in Chinese and Japanese Zen. As the Japanese Zen master Hakuin said, "This very place is the Lotus Land, and this very body is the Buddha."

The *Lotus* gospel is no more one of salvation by faith than is the Early Buddhist teaching. Acts of faith, making vows, and affirmations of commitment lead to hearing the Dharma. The works of the devotee and the gifts of the teacher-savior are equally indispensible parts of an interaction cycle. In Mahāyāna as in Hīnayāna, the Buddhas are preeminently teachers and revealers. They do not grant mundane favors such as children for the childless, wealth for the poor, and rescue from danger.

Akṣobhya is the earliest attested of the nonhistorical celestial Buddhas. In the *Vimalakīrti,* Gautama says: "There is a country named Abhirati and a Buddha named Akṣobhya. This Vimalakīrti died in that country and came to birth here." To satisfy the assembly's longing, Vimalakīrti entered samādhi, and grasped Abhirati and set it down in this world to be seen. Afterward it returned to its proper place, in the East. In the *Small Prajñā-pāramitā,* Śākyamuni exerts his wonder-working power and enables his assembly to see Akṣobhya and his retinue. Neither Sūtra advocates devotion to Akṣobhya. Apparently, though, rebirth in Abhirati was sought by some people. It could be attained through moral acts, or even through hearing the name of Akṣobhya. This Buddha became moderately popular in Tantrism. In art he is represented as blue, holding a *vajra* ("thunderbolt") in his right hand, his left hand in the earth-witness gesture, with a blue elephant for his mount. The name Akṣobhya means "immovable" or "imperturbable." Legend says that while he was just a bodhisattva he made a vow to practice deeds without anger. The bodhisattva who does likewise will go to birth in Abhirati.

Amitābha ("Unlimited Light") and *Amitāyus* ("Unlimited Lifespan") are alternate names for the same Buddha. Chinese A-mi-t'o and Japanese Amida transliterate a short form, Amita. The cult of this Buddha goes back at least to 100 A.D.

We have seen that the origin legends of the celestial bodhisattvas are vague, synthetic-looking, and subject to conflicting versions. By contrast, the Amitābha legend is specific, furnished with history-like detail, and unified. Successive Chinese translations of the *Sukhāvatī-vyūha Sūtra,* and the late Sanskrit text which survives, show significant variations, but they exhibit a consistent pattern of development. The later the version, the more Amitābha is glorified as against Śākyamuni, and the fewer the restrictions on his power.

Countless kalpas ago a bhikṣu named Dharmākara ("Mine or Treasury of Dharma") heard the Buddha Lokeśvararāja preach, and expressed a fervent desire to become a Buddha like him. He implored the Buddha to teach him the way to supreme perfect enlightenment and the qualities of a pure Buddha-field. The Tathāgata then taught him for ten million years the excellences and amenities of innumerable Buddha-lands. Dharmākara took all these good qualities, concentrated them all on one Buddha-land, and meditated on them for five kalpas. Then he went to his future Buddha-land. The number of these vows varies from twenty-four in the earliest versions to forty-eight in the later.

In his Buddha-field, said Dharmākara, there will be no evil destinies (hell, animals, ghosts, asuras). In other words, everyone born there will be at least a stream-winner (see p. 27). There will only be a nominal difference between men and gods in that Buddha-land. All beings born there will be almost but not quite arhants. They will all be destined for consummation in nirvāṇa, and unless their bodhisattva vows bind them to more rebirths, they will only be reborn once. But their lifespan in Sukhāvatī ("Happiness-having") will be unlimited. Evil will not be known there even by name. All beings there will be able to hear automatically whatever Dharma-theme they wish, but there will be neither teaching nor learning, because all will possess direct cognition and will be able to recite the Dharma informed by all-knowledge.

The Buddha Amita will have unlimited light and unlimited life. His congregation of disciples will be countless, and innumerable Tathāgatas in other Buddha-lands will proclaim his fame and praise. In return, bodhisattvas from Sukhāvatī will travel everywhere to visit and worship the other Buddhas, while beings who stay in Sukhāvatī have merely to think of making offerings to Buddhas elsewhere and the gifts will automatically spring into being and be accepted. Bodhisattvas in that country will be able at will to convert their merit into precious substances, incense, robes, umbrellas, flags, lamps, dancing, and music. Just by wishing, the bodhisattvas will produce masses of superb ornaments from the jewel trees of the land. There will be a myriad incense burners always emitting fragrance.

Dharmākara, when he becomes a Buddha, will exercise tremendous outreach. Other Buddhas everywhere will declare his name and fame, and from hearing his name living beings will derive manifold benefit. Women who hear the name of Amita will never again be reborn as women. (This is not just masculine arrogance, but a judgment on women's life in ancient Asia with which women generally concurred.) Living beings in other Buddha-lands who hear Amita's name will be released from birth and gain knowledge of the *dhāraṇīs* ("spells"). Through hearing his name they will attain birth in a noble family. Bodhisattvas who hear Amita's name will be honored by gods and men if they worship him. They will attain a samādhi in which they dwell continually seeing countless Buddhas, until they reach bodhi. They will earn merit by rejoicing in the bodhisattva course. No bodhisattva who hears Amita's name will ever relapse or forsake the Three Jewels.

The most crucial question concerning a Buddha-land is how to attain rebirth there. Dharmākara's vows answer specifically, though different versions of the Sūtra vary significantly. The second-century Chinese translation says that if someone who has aroused the thought of bodhi always meditates on Amita with a faith-filled mind, then when he dies Amita and his retinue will come to meet him and escort him to Sukhāvatī. On the other hand, those who have done evil in former lives, if they hear Amita's name and sincerely aspire to birth in his land, will when they die not go to bad destinies but be reborn in Sukhāvatī.

The third-century translation distinguishes three classes of candidates for rebirth: evildoers, good Buddhists, and practicing bodhisattvas. The general prerequisites for rebirth are a desire to be reborn there and good conduct (with dedication of the resultant merit to rebirth and bodhi). The sinner must hear Amita's name, and must repent and reform. The ordinary devotee must perform worship and donation. The bodhisattva must meditate, presumably upon Amitābha and his paradise. Note that faith is not mentioned at all.

In the Chinese version adopted as orthodox by the Chinese and Japanese Pure Land sects, the eighteenth vow says that all living beings in the ten directions who with sincere faith desire rebirth in Amita's country, calling this desire to mind even ten times, will attain it. Only those who have committed atrocities or slandered the True Dharma are excluded. The nineteenth vow says that all living beings in the ten directions who arouse the thought of bodhi, cultivate all the virtues, and wholeheartedly vow to be reborn in Amita's country will, when they die, see Amita and a large retinue before them. The twentieth vow says that if living beings in the ten directions hear Amita's name, fix their thoughts on his country (that is, meditate on it), plant all the roots of virtue, and wholeheartedly dedicate (the resulting merit) desiring rebirth in his country, then it will happen that way. Here the general prerequisites are a desire for rebirth, and good conduct. (Presumably dedication of merit is required by all three vows.) No distinction is made between classes of devotees. One may meditate with sincere faith as little as ten times. Or one may arouse the thought of bodhi. Or one may hear Amita's name and meditate on his country. But faith alone is not stated to suffice for rebirth.

The foregoing excursion into textual criticism has been necessary because the whole edifice of Far Eastern Pure Land dogmatics rests on the interpretation of these three vows. The issue is whether salvation requires both faith and works, or faith alone. On the evidence of the Sūtra in all surviving versions, faith is just an adjunct of meditation. The concentrated, aspiring mind is faith-filled. Salvation, furthermore, is not effected by Amita's power alone. The candidate, too, must make an effort. The Buddha's name is a talisman for those who lack merit, but in the early and detailed third-century translation, the sacred name alone does not cancel one's sins; repentance and reform are needed, too. In India the Amitābha cult was a religion of devout contemplation rather than of pure faith. It was a road to salvation not through "Other-power," but through the cooperation of Amitābha's supervening power and the devotee's own exertions.

Having proclaimed his vows, Dharmākara practiced the bodhisattva course for a trillion years. He established innumerable living beings in supreme perfect enlightenment. He worshipped countless Buddhas. Gradually his body became transformed, a sweet scent issued from his mouth and pores, and he acquired the signs and marks of a Great Person. Finally, ten kalpas ago, he became the Tathāgata Amitābha presiding over the world-realm Sukhāvatī, a trillion Buddha-fields away to the West, which is endowed with all the virtues he had vowed that it would have.

The Buddha-lands differ from the heavens of the gods in that they are presided over by a Buddha, so that the inhabitants can practice the way, earn merit, and gain wisdom. In the heavens of the gods, a nonreturner can attain arhant-ship only through the maturing of merit he had previously earned as a human being. But the appurtenances of the celestial Buddha-lands are very much like those of the deva-worlds. The inhabitants of both are freed from labor, and the necessities of life come to them for the mere wishing. Sex is attenuated or entirely eliminated, and birth takes place without coitus or gestation.

The pure Buddha-lands differ from the Iranian, Christian, and Muslim paradises in that their delights are a means to the goal of bodhi rather than an end in themselves. All who go to Sukhāvatī are assured that they will attain enlightenment there, but residence in the Happy Land is neither an equivalent nor a substitute for nirvāṇa. Some inhabitants of Amita's land are disciples, and they become arhants and enter parinirvāṇa, which of course is not localized in any world-realm. Others are bodhisattvas, and being bound by their vows, when they attain the highest stage they do not enter cessation, but appear at will throughout all the worlds in order to benefit living beings.

Vairocana ("shining out") is an epithet of the sun, and was originally just an epithet of Śākyamuni, but in due course acquired separate identity as a celestial Buddha. In the Tantric set of the Five Tathāgatas, he occupies the center, which is Śākyamuni's position in the exoteric Mahāyāna maṇḍala. The Chinese scholastic view that Vairocana is the Dharmakāya of Śākyamuni thus reaffirms the identity from which Vairocana had historically been derived.

We have seen that solar traits characterize the early accounts of Śākyamuni's enlightenment (pp. 18–19). Ignorance was paired with darkness, and knowledge with light. Daybreak and the Enlightenment were synchronized. The *Lotus Sūtra* represents the Buddha's revealing act as a beam of light shooting from the "wisdom-eye" between his brows. Amitābha's very name signifies that he is a luminary deity, and his Buddha-land is suffused with radiance in all the hues of the rainbow. It is a land of eternal daylight, devoid of shadows.

The *Mahāvairocana Sūtra,* a Tantric work composed in about the seventh century, consists of Vairocana's revelations to the Tantric equivalents of Bodhisattvas. The venue of the Sūtra is frankly nonterrestrial: the residence of Śiva at the top of the form realm.

Vairocana did not become popular either in art or in cult until the seventh century, when his role as Śākyamuni's transcendental counterpart gave him preeminence in the Tantric cosmoplans (maṇḍalas) and the associated rites.

The Doctrine of Mind Only

We have seen that mind and consciousness (*vijñāna*) occupied a unique place in early Buddhism. It is vijñāna that transmigrates, it is in his mind-made body that the adept travels through the heavens, and the gods in the highest heavens have bodies that are made of mind only. The power of mind was proverbial. "All dharmas are forerun by mind, chieftained by mind, consist of mind" (Dh. 1). "Those who restrain mind, which is far-ranging, walks alone, is bodiless, and sits in the cave of the heart, will be freed from the bonds of death" (Dh. 37). This concept of mind is much closer to the ātman of the Upaniṣads than to the six consciousnesses each specialized to one sense into which Early Buddhist doctrine fragmented the mind. It is sometimes said to be intrinsically pure: "This mind is luminous, but sometimes it is soiled by extraneous defilements."

The Śūnyavādins were not concerned with the phenomenology of mind, but in asserting that all phenomena are illusion (*māyā*), cinematic fictions, and dreamlike, they accorded the mind a major role in creating the seeming world. Conventional things, they said, are not purely objective entities but concepts or discriminations constructed by the mind under the influence of ignorance. This raises several questions that the Śūnyavādins did not answer. What, in worldly scientific terms, is the process by which the mind creates and objectifies fictions? What is the real nature of error? If the sense-consciousnesses arise and perish moment by moment following their evanescent objects, which of them figments the objects, and how is the process of world construction passed on from moment to moment? How do memories take place? And what is it that experiences the absolute truth free from discrimination?

The attempt to answer such questions gave rise to a new school called Yogācāra ("Yoga Practice") or Vijñānavāda ("Consciousnessism"). Its doctrines appeared first in several Sūtras about 300 A.D.: the *Avataṃsaka,* the *Sandhinirmocana,* and the *Laṅkāvatāra.* The earliest Vijñānavādin treatises are attributed to Maitreyanātha, who may have been either a human philosopher or the Bodhisattva. He inspired the two brothers Asaṅga and Vasubandhu (c. fourth century) who commented on his treatises and brought the school to its definitive form.

The Sautrāntikas (as noted on p. 40) maintained that the effects of deeds are transmitted as a series of "seeds" until they ripen. The Yogācāra school named this stream of "seeds" the *ālaya-vijñāna* ("store or foundation consciousness"). They treated the *manas* ("mind") as a defiled consciousness intermediate between the store-consciousness and the six sense-consciousnesses, and thus established a set of eight vijñānas.

The store-consciousness is inactive, but the other seven consciousnesses are active. The ālaya and the manas are unconscious, while the other six are conscious, that is, aware of objects. The ālaya-vijñāna is not a substance like the Upaniṣadic ātman, though. It is simply a series of seeds, each momentary, each giving rise to its successor. It contains not only defiled seeds, but pure dharmas which somewhat mysteriously emanate from the pure Dharma-dhātu to imbue living beings with virtue. As the person progresses toward enlightenment, the defilements are gradually eliminated and displaced by pure dharmas until finally there occurs a "revolution of the personality-base." As the *Laṅkāvatāra* says, "Through fully knowing that external things are shown by one's own mind, there occurs the revolution at the personality-base of discrimination, which is liberation and not destruction."

The Vijñānavādin Sūtras (*Laṅkavatāra, Śrīmālā-devīsiṃhanāda,* and so on) equate the ālaya-vijñāna with the *tathāgata-garbha,* a concept of great soteriological importance. *Garbha* has a twofold general meaning: first, the womb, and by extension, an inner room, the calyx of a lotus; and second, the womb's contents, that is, an embryo, fetus, child. In the first sense, the purified store-consciousness is the womb where the tathāgata is conceived and nourished and matured. The *Wisdom Sūtras* had already introduced the uteral metaphor when they declared that Prajñā Pāramitā is the mother of all the Buddhas (see p. 57). The new term just makes it more physiological. In the second sense, the tathāgata-garbha is the embryonic Buddha consisting of the pure dharmas in a person's ālaya-vijñāna. The *Lotus Sūtra* proclaims that the Buddha will enable all beings to attain final nirvāṇa, but does not examine the implicit idea that every living being harbors the capability or potentiality of Buddhahood.

The later Sūtras originating in India specify that the germ of Tathāgatahood is innate to all living beings, since they are irradiated by the pervading power of the Buddha, and since through time without beginning they have grown a stock of good dharmas under the influence of this radiating grace. If this germ did not exist, a person could not take religious initiative, could not turn from transmigration and aspire to nirvāṇa. This germ is always intrinsically pure, and is synonymous with suchness, which is identical in everyone. In ordinary beings, it is covered with adventitious impurities; in the bodhisattvas, it is partly pure and partly impure; and in the Buddhas, it is perfectly pure.

The tathāgata-garbha is described in a series of similes. It is like the Buddha in a faded lotus, like honey covered by bees, like a kernel of grain in the husk, like gold in the ore, like a treasure hidden in the earth, like the fruit in a small seed, like a Buddha-image wrapped in rags, like a great king in the womb of a low-caste woman, and like a precious statue covered with dirt. These similes fall roughly into two classes, the organic and the mineral. Of the former, two imply growth: the small seed grows into a fruit tree, and the fetus grows into a great king. Most of the similes connote an immutable thing that will emerge unstained when it is unwrapped or washed. It is no wonder that the *Laṅkāvatāra* has to protest that the tathāgata-garbha is not the same as the Hindu ātman. To the ordinary person, gems and gold and statues are enduring things, as close to eternal immutables as a commonsense example can come.

The tathāgata-garbha contains the causes from which pure as well as impure dharmas arise. It is the source of the phenomenal world, of good things and bad alike. This follows from its office as storeroom for the seeds of past karma. But since the tathāgata-garbha is synonymous with the Dharmakāya of the Buddha, this leads in a tortuous way to the conclusion that the Buddha creates the world. For centuries the Buddhists had been striving to avoid conceding their ultimate entity (nirvāṇa, suchness, Dharma-dhātu, tathāgata) the role of an agent (see p. 38). Embarrassed Vijñānavādins insisting that their theory of individual and cosmic genesis is different from the Brāhmanical creation theories sound rather like East European Communists in the late 1960's protesting that adoption of the profit principle and market-responsive pricing does not mean they are turning to capitalism. In both instances, the advantageous features borrowed from rival systems are subordinated and integrated without sacrificing the essential characteristics of the established structures. But this fact is easy for the unsympathetic critic to overlook.

Earlier Buddhist schools had dealt awkwardly and unsatisfactorily with the facts of psychic continuity. They had restricted the six sense-consciousnesses to witnessing present objects, and so had disqualified them as regents of memory. Vijñānavāda introduced two extra consciousnesses which between them have charge of storing the impressions deposited by experiences, and projecting them into new events when they ripen. This explanation was applied to memory, the continuity of personality through sleep and deep trance, and the transmission of identity between successive lives.

The store-consciousness is both individual and collective. It receives the impressions of individual deeds, harbors them, and projects the phenomenal world, consisting of: (1) the "receptacle world" of space-time, and (2) the psychophysical individual. The purified mind of the saint no longer projects a phenomenal world of its own, but it sees the world projected by the minds of ignorant people.

Whereas Mādhyamika posits two "truths," the relative and the absolute, Yogācāra sets up three "natures" (*svabhāva*), the absolute, the relative, and the imaginary. Practice of the path purges the imaginary out of the relative and so refines it into the absolute. Mādhyamika ridicules the idea of a coupling of the real and the unreal, but this is just what the Yogācārin relative nature is. Furthermore, the imaginary has its basis in the absolute. After all, where else could illusion have its source except in reality?

The Yogācāra introduced the doctrine of the three bodies of the Buddha. The first is the *nirmāṇa-kāya* ("apparition-body"), which corresponds to the nirmāṇa-kāya and rūpa-kāya of the earlier teachings. The third is the Dharmakāya. The second is a Yogācārin innovation, the *Sambhoga-kāya* ("Body of recompense, or enjoyment"). It is the glorified body that the Buddha attains as a reward for his bodhisattva practices, and it is the transfigured body which the great bodhisattvas apprehend when they see the Buddha. For example, Amitābha in his Pure Land is apprehended in his *Sambhoga-kāya* by the bodhisattvas there, while he appears in his Nirmāṇa-kāya to favored persons in this world.

Vasubandhu, coarchitect of the Yogācāra system, was also the greatest of the Abhidharmists. For better or worse, the new school took over the Abhidharma enterprise, pulled together all the classifications, subclassifications, lists, and numbers that appeared in the Sūtras and treatises, and with greater zeal than good sense proceeded to invent more and more. The system became very unwieldy, and provided an occupation for monks with plenty of time who would rather study than practice. There is, nonetheless, a sort of religious exaltation to be derived from contemplating this architectonic scholastic edifice; and, since Vasubandhu and Asaṅga wrote short and fairly clear summaries of their system, those who wanted to bypass the luxuriant detail could do so.

The Vajrayāna

Two of the basic components of the *Vajrayāna* ("Thunderbolt or Diamond Vehicle") were present in Buddhism long before the Tantric movement became prominent in the seventh century A.D. Magic spells occur in the Mahāyāna Sūtras as early as 200 A.D. By the seventh century, though, Buddhism had incorporated the Hindu notion of inherently efficacious sounds (such as OṂ), and had elaborated a set of magic syllables, associating one with each major figure in the Tantric pantheon and with each "center" in the mystic physiology. The second feature, the maṇḍala or sacred circle, derives many of its features from religious architecture. Early stūpas, with their railings separating sacred and profane ground, were intended as replicas of the cosmos. When the Buddha-image came into use about 100 A.D., images were placed at the cardinal points of the stūpa or the courtyard surrounding it. The shrine thus became a three-dimensional maṇḍala.

The Tantric innovation was to turn the creation of maṇḍalas into an "actualization," a rite in which the agent becomes the deity whom he conjures up. Maṇḍalas can be made in painting, in three-dimensional models, by a troupe dramatically acting it out, or by a yogin visualizing the setting and the figures. Such rites were foreign to both Hīnayāna and Mahāyāna, but they had a venerable Brāhmanical ancestry. The rationale of Vedic sacrifice was much the same, and we even read of a fire sacrifice that would impart immortality. The highest purpose of Tantric actualizations, though, is attainment of enlightenment, the regular Buddhist goal.

Enough has been said to demonstrate that Vajrayāna, the "Thunderbolt Vehicle," represented the culmination of trends long present in Buddhism. But it was also a radical departure from the classical tradition. The basic layer of the new cult seems to have been witchcraft. Imagine a Bengali or Assamese cemetery at night, in the year 600. Eight corpses are arranged in a circle, and a ninth is set in the center. A naked low-caste girl is standing or sitting on each of the corpses. In the center there is a man wearing a tiara of human skulls on his head, girt with a girdle of human hair, his body smeared with ashes, holding in one hand a trident adorned with a human skull, and with the other hand beating a drum. The coven dances, sings, chants spells, drinks wine, eats human flesh, and copulates.

At some time, renegade Buddhist monks either joined such witches' covens or imitated them. In the hands of men who, however they violated the precepts, still sought the Buddhist goal, these rites were imbued with doctrinal significance and converted into a sacramental means of realization. These masters systematized the rites and eventually wrote them down in the form of *Tantras* ("Manuals"). The Tantras were intended as aids for initiants training under a master. They were not for public perusal, and their secrets were safeguarded by an argot called "twilight speech" in which, for example, semen was called "camphor," "the thought of bodhi," and "elixir"; the male and female genitals were called "thunderbolt" and "lotus"; and the corpse of an executed criminal was called a "banner."

It is not surprising that Vajrayāna has been excoriated by many modern writers. It has been said that Tantrism was a degeneration, that it grafted the Hindu cult of female energies onto Buddhism, and that the graft became a parasite which in due course crushed the life out of its host.

What happened was in fact the reverse. The main Buddhist tradition assimilated the witch cult, appropriating its elements, restructuring and reinterpreting them, until it would be more correct to say that pure Buddhism crushed the life out of the Tantras. By 800 A.D., Tantric studies had achieved the dignity of an academic discipline. Learned scholars in Bengal and Bihar were writing commentaries, giving glosses for the "twilight language," explaining the symbolic meanings of the ritual objects, persons, and acts, and suffusing the subject with a refined and ethical tone. The practitioners who wrote the Tantras considered that the accompanying mental acts were more important than the physical acts of the rites. It was a commonplace that everything is mind-only, so it was not always necessary to perform the rites physically. The yogin could call up the visions in his mind and perform the rites in imagination. After a time, most Tantric schools ceased to perform those rites which infringed the precepts. Vajrayāna became respectable, and shifted from orgies to exercises in pure contemplation.

Tantric practice is based on the Mādhyamika principle that saṃsāra and nirvāṇa are not different. As Nāgārjuna said, "The limit of saṃsāra is the limit of nirvāṇa. Between these two there is not even the subtlest something." Also, "Unrelated to the pure there is nothing impure with reference to which we can designate the pure. Therefore even the pure is not a matter of fact." An early Buddhist maxim says: "Living beings are defiled through defilement of the mind, and purified through purification of the mind."

The Tantric poet Saraha says, "Here there's no beginning, no middle, no end, no saṃsāra, no nirvāṇa. In this state of supreme bliss, there's no self and no other." "Just as water entering water becomes of the same taste, so when the sage thinks vices and virtues the same, there's no polarity." In other words, the enlightened man is beyond good and evil.

The crux of the matter is skill in means. The *Hevajra Tantra* says, "The unknowing worldling who drinks strong poison is overpowered; he who has expelled delusion, with his mind on the truth, destroys it utterly." What is licit under the direction of a guru and within the consecrated maṇḍala is still illicit for ordinary people. When the tabus are broken, they must be broken with a pure mind and not for worldly pleasure.

The aim of the Tantric devotee is to destroy the passions by means of the passions. As the *Hevajra* says, "The expert in poison repells poison by that very poison, a little bit of which kills most people. . . . Those who have 'means' are liberated from the bondage of 'becoming' through the very thing by which wicked people are bound. The world is bound by lust, and released by the same lust."

Who should ritually break the tabus, and who should not? Tantric doctrine classifies people into five "tribes" or "families" according to personality type, and prescribes a different method for each tribe. Classical manuals recommended different meditations depending on the student's dominant passion. The lust type should meditate on impurity, the hostility type on compassion, and the folly type on causal relations. Tantric lore incorporated this and combined it with the schema of the Five Tathāgatas. The classical prescription for the hostility type is cultivation of compassion and friendly love. Tantrism prescribes for him the performance of erotic rites. "Compassion" is twilight speech for "sexual love." Vajrayāna fuses spiritual and physical love, in idea and in practice.

One of the most basic Mahāyāna pairs is wisdom (*prajñā*) and means (*upāya*). Wisdom soon became a goddess (see p. 57). The Tantras made Means a male divinity. The union of Wisdom and Means produces the Thought of Bodhi. In the maṇḍala of Hevajra, the goddess Nairātmyā ("No-self") stands for Wisdom, and Hevajra stands for Means. When the maṇḍala is acted out, the yogin impersonates Hevajra, and his consort takes the part of Nairātmyā.

The rites are practiced long and thoroughly in contemplation before they are actually performed. The yogin imagines the maṇḍala and the goddesses around the circle, and mentally envisages the rites with himself as the deity. Having conjured up this vivid drama, he contemplates that these phenomena, like all others, are empty, that there is neither subject nor object, neither thought nor thinker.

Such visualizations are a considerable psychological feat. Images and paintings are used to support the imagination, and in turn the artist pictures the themes in his mind before executing the painting or the statue.

The body, which earlier Buddhism tended to devalue in one way or another, received its due in Vajrayāna. Saraha says: "Here's the Jumna, river of gods, and here's the Ganges' flood; here are Prayāga and Benares, here are the Moon and Sun. In wandering, I've visited all kinds of Tantric meeting-places, but never have I seen another holy place as blissful as my body." Tantric physiology is mystical rather than anatomical. It confounds the circulation and nervous systems, for example. It posits four psychic centers (navel, heart, throat, and brain) and three main channels, one corresponding to the spinal column and the other two to the jugular veins. It says that the Thought of Enlightenment ascends at the moment of Great Bliss (orgasm) until it reaches the highest center.

The Tantras do not in fact advocate murder, even ritually, and they observe the general Buddhist prohibition against animal sacrifice, which Hinduism allowed as an exception to its precept against injuring sentient things. But the Tantras do enjoin illicit and even incestuous sexual relations, and they do prescribe drinking wine and eating the flesh of men, cows, elephants, horses, and dogs. Early Buddhism was not vegetarian, but during the fourth century A.D. Mahāyāna adopted vegetarianism from the Hindus. Cowslaughter had become a heinous crime by Tantric times, so for an upper-caste Indian, whether Brāhman or Buddhist, eating beef was virtually as repugnant as cannibalism.

The effectiveness of the Tantric path is witnessed by the great saints it produced. Each major Buddhist movement has created its own type of holy man and incited the zeal of its followers by pointing to living exemplars. In the Buddha's day, many attained arhant-ship. As the generations went by, the ideal faded and fewer attained it. Then in early Mahāyāna the bodhisattva path offered human saints of modest attainment fellowship with the celestial bodhisattvas. But the latter were so extolled that they eventually robbed earthly bodhisattva-hood of all glamor. Seventh-century China circumvented the scholastic claptrap concerning the bodhisattva course and created a new type of holy man in the Zen master. The Tantric *siddhas* ("accomplished ones") combined features from most of the preceding Indian types of wizard and saint, and added some new traits, both bizarre and admirable. They usually lived and operated outside the regular monastic communities, which continued their old style of life throughout the Tantric period. Some Tantric adepts were bhikṣus, but some, too, were householders. They were recruited from all castes and classes, and they wandered around the country, mixing freely with outcastes and tribals, begging from door to door, frequenting cremation grounds and haunted places. They trafficked with demons and took outcaste girls for their ritual consorts. Some achieved success with very little instruction, and some went through many years of ordeals under stern and capricious masters. The one great rule for the Tantric student was absolute obedience and devotion to his guru, whom he must worship as a very Buddha. Success depended on the guru's ability to "psych out" the student's problems and states of mind, manipulate him through personal interaction, and use charisma to overcome blocks that the student could not surmount by himself. The Tantric guru is thus a variant of the pan-Buddhist teacher-savior type.

The Extinction of Buddhism in India

In the seventh century, Buddhism was fairly strong in most parts of India. Hsüan-tsang reported quite a few deserted monasteries here and there, but prospering centers were numerous and widely distributed. Archaeology tells the tale of a steady decline over the next several centuries in most regions. After 600, Buddhism in the South gradually gave way to the devotional Hinduism of the Tamil minstrel saints. It left its influence on Tamil theism, however, fostering the idea of a compassionate God; native Dravidian culture was bloodthirsty and not very prone to mercy or compassion. Kāñcīpuram (Conjeeveram) was a renowned Buddhist center, and as late as the fifteenth century a Theravāda community existed there.

The White Hun invasions in the sixth century devastated the monasteries of Gandhāra, but Buddhism continued to prosper in nearby Kashmir, where by the ninth century, though, Buddhism and Śaivism became intermingled. Muslim rulers finally stamped out Kashmiri Buddhism during the course of the fifteenth century. In Sindh, the Ganges valley, and Orissa, Buddhism flourished until the Muslim invaders sacked the monasteries and butchered the monks. Nālandā was pillaged and burned in 1198, and though it continued to function on a reduced scale for several decades, repeated attacks by Muslim marauders eventually exterminated the institution. Buddhism lingered for a couple centuries as a folk cult in Bihar, Bengal, and Orissa, then disappeared.

It has been said that Buddhism disappeared from India because it was imprudently tolerant and gradually became so Hinduized that it lost all reason for a separate existence. This is at best a partial truth. Mahāyāna was quite hostile to theistic Hinduism. The householder bodhisattva pledged himself never on pain of death to worship Viṣṇu and Śiva. Āryadeva reportedly entered a South Indian temple and tore the eye out of a baleful idol of Śiva. The mutual antipathy was still evident about 1000 A.D., when a Bengali Brāhman family strongly opposed the marriage of their daughter to Nāropa, who came from a Buddhist family. A Kashmiri play of the same general period takes the rivalry among Buddhism, Jainism, and various Hindu sects as its theme. It evinces both a strong sense of the distinctions between sects, and a genial spirit of conciliation. The element of truth in this theory is that institutional Buddhism had grown self-centered, conservative, and unresponsive to the needs of the people. The great monasteries depended not on widows' mites but on landed estates and royal grants, so they neglected to maintain popular support, became divorced from the rural populace; and when the monasteries lost royal support, or were destroyed by invasions, the general population had little interest in either preserving the Dharma or restoring the Saṅgha.

It is not unnatural that Buddhism should have died out in India. Mithraism and Manicheism, widespread and powerful in their day, perished, yet scholars are not overly amazed. The Vedic religion died about the time that Buddhism arose, Christianity vanished gradually from its Oriental homelands under Muslim occupation, and in this century Confucianism has ceased to be a religion. From very early, Indian Buddhists had expected the Dharma eventually to decline and disappear. Though Buddhism in its homeland finally went the way of all conditioned things, it had by then lighted the lamp of the Dharma in many other parts of Asia, and had endured several times as long as any empire that has ever held sway in India.

4.
Developments Outside India

China

In the first century A.D., the new and strong Later Han dynasty extended Chinese power into Central Asia again, where the various small kingdoms owed their prosperity to the silk trade between China and the West. Serindian merchant colonies—Khotanese, Sogdians, Parthians, Kucheans, and Kuṣāṇas—settled in an arc of cities from Tun-huang in the northwest to the Huai valley. Their families often stayed in China for generations, and became bilingual and bicultural. As some of these people were Buddhists, they welcomed and accommodated the monks who traveled with the caravans. The Chinese, despite their fabled antipathy to learning from foreigners, have always loved exotica; and no doubt the orange-robed śramaṇas filled them with the same kind of wonder as parakeets from Cambodia and horses from Ferghana. China has also cherished throughout the ages an addiction to magic, and the men of Han promptly recognized the kinship between the bhikṣu and the indigenous shaman and wizard-hermit. By the mid-century, Chinese patricians were giving dāna feasts, and śramaṇas were a familiar sight in the capital.

The first notable translator, the Parthian An Shih-kao, arrived in 148 at Lo-yang, the capital, where he worked for twenty years translating short treatises on meditation and Abhidharma. The first known Chinese monk was his disciple, and the beginnings of Buddhist literature in Chinese went hand in hand with the formation of a Chinese Saṅgha.

Lokakṣema, the first known Mahāyāna missionary, worked in Lo-yang between 168 and 188. He translated the *Small Perfect Wisdom Sūtra* and the *Sukhāvatī-vyūha* (see p. 66). The cult of Amita made no impression at that time, but Chinese familiar with Chuang-tzu were intrigued by Prajñā thought and demanded fresh translations of the Sūtras from each successive missionary, though it was not until the early fifth century that they really understood Śūnyavāda.

The Later Han regime fell apart during the latter half of the second century. As magic is commonly the resort of the desperate, many of the gentry soon followed the path the peasants had taken decades earlier, and sought strength and security in the occult. Their interest in Buddhism at this time focused on meditation as a means of obtaining paranormal powers. Only some of these gentlemen became monks; others served as scribes and assistants to the foreign monks, or practiced dhyāna as lay recluses.

The work of translation and evangelization continued through the third century and came to fruition in the Western Chin period (265–316). Dharmarakṣa, "the bodhisattva from Tun-huang," worked in North China from 266 to 308. Under him the Chinese Saṅgha reached the takeoff point. His disciples established monasteries, lectured on the Sūtras, ordained monks, and proselytized vigorously. The sacking of the capitals at the end of Western Chin served to disperse Dharmarakṣa's school to other parts of the country and thus disseminate the new vigorous and intellectual style of Buddhism. The process was repeated often during the centuries of political division. Monasteries and libraries were often burned, but what the Saṅgha lost in security it gained in mobility and communication.

The monks in South China under Eastern Chin (317–419) lived peacefully and gradually insinuated themselves into the highest gentry circles by adroit use of literary wit and personal urbanity. In the North, monks lived dangerously under the rule of "barbarian" chieftains, among a mixed population of Chinese, Tibetans, and Altaic tribesmen. The brave and righteous old Kuchean wonder-worker Fo-t'u-teng became court adviser to the Hunnish state of Later Chao, mitigated the excesses of its rulers, and trained a cadre of disciplined and enterprising Chinese monks.

Tao-an (312–385) was the most illustrious of Fo-t'u-teng's disciples. Though driven from place to place by the incessant civil wars, he lectured on the Prajñā Sūtras, collected copies of the scriptures and prepared the first catalog of them, invited foreign monks and supported their translation work, and promoted devotion to Maitreya.

His disciple Hui-yüan (334–416/417) ran a school for gentleman monks and scholars in which he reinterpreted the Confucian and Taoist classics in a Buddhist sense, encouraged the writing of Buddhist devotional poetry in a typical Chinese style, and founded a society for meditation on Amitābha. He settled on Mount Lu and spent the last thirty years of his life there, letting the world come to him (as it did), and the armies pass him by. He staunchly defended the autonomy of the Saṅgha against the state, insisting that the śramaṇa is not obliged to kowtow to the ruler.

Thanks to the efforts of Tao-an and Hui-yüan, a sizable intellectual elite in the Saṅgha was ready to receive the great Kuchean translator Kumārajīva (344–413) when he reached Ch'ang-an in 401. With the patronage of the King of Ch'in, Kumārajīva and a large team of Chinese collaborators retranslated the most popular Sūtras done by his predecessors and translated four Mādhyamika treatises, introducing Nāgārjuna's teachings to the Chinese. His translations were elegant and intelligible, though not always accurate. To this day they are in general use, in preference to the more accurate translations of Hsüan-tsang (*c.* 596–664).

The three generations of Chinese intellectual monks from Tao-an to Kumārajīva's disciples are called the Buddho-Taoists, because they discussed Buddhism in a Taoist vocabulary and sought in Buddhism solutions to Neo-Taoist problems such as the relation of the Holy Man to the world, whether he acts, and whether he feels compassion. The last luminary in this movement was Kumārajīva's young disciple Seng-chao (374–414). His four surviving essays are outstanding expressions of Śūnyavāda in Chinese vocabulary and literary form. Kumārajīva's school was dispersed when the Ch'in kingdom fell. Some of his disciples fled south, and a few went west to the warlord state in Kansu.

Throughout the fifth and early sixth centuries, North and South China pursued separate courses, the South under native dynasties and the North under "barbarian" rulers. Southern Buddhists continued literary activity, producing new translations, debating doctrinal issues, lecturing, and commenting on the principal Sūtras.

Northern Buddhism during the fifth century excelled in works rather than ideas. Intellectual laymen and monks had mostly fled south when the "barbarian" Northern Wei (386–534) conquered Ch'in and seized Ch'ang-an in 418. The founder of this dynasty favored Buddhism, forbade his troops to pillage the Saṅgha's premises, and ordered the officers in his capital to erect Buddha-images and provide dwellings for monks. He appointed a moral and learned monk to the civil service post of Saṅgha-director, thus establishing government jurisdiction over the monasteries in his realm. The monk appointed did not fight, as Hui-yüan did in the South, for the independence of the Saṅgha from the state, but kowtowed to the emperor and justified this seeming contravention of the monastic rule by identifying the emperor with the Tathāgata!

Buddhism flourished and spread in Northern Wei until excessive prosperity led to corruption within the Saṅgha and intrigues by jealous Taoists and Confucians. In 446 an edict decreed the destruction of Sūtras, images, and paintings, and the execution of monks. Many monks were able to go into hiding, taking Sūtras and images with them; but many temples and scriptures were destroyed, and some monks were put to death.

A new emperor decreed an end to the proscription in 454. From then on, Northern Wei rulers patronized Buddhism lavishly, and employed monks in responsible civil service posts.

Shortly after 460, the Saṅgha director persuaded the emperor to undertake one of the world's great religious monuments, the cave temples of Yün-kang. Twenty grottoes were excavated in a limestone cliff several miles from the capital, Ta-t'ung. The earliest caves contain giant stone Buddha-images, while the walls of later ones are sculptured profusely with scenes from the Sūtras, the life of the Buddha, bodhisattvas, devas, gandharvas, apsarases, and human donors. The project was an act of expiation for the persecution of Buddhism, an indication of imperial favor to the religion, and an attempt to create an expression of the Dharma that would withstand the ravages of time and persecution.

Chinese Buddhism, both Northern and Southern, became sectarian during the sixth century. It should be noted that though Chinese *tsung* is translated "sect" or "school," it denotes a wider range of institutions than either English word. In the classics *tsung* means "clan shrine; clan." Buddhists borrowed the terminology. A tsung consists of people who trace their Dharma-descent to a common *tsu* ("ancestor, founder, patriarch").

One sign that Buddhism was acculturating to China in the sixth century was the interest shown by great masters in tracing their lineage back to Śākyamuni. To do this, they had to eke out and cobble together Indian lists and names, sometimes filling the gaps with outright fabrications. The felt need was evidently acute. In Chinese eyes, a teaching was vouched for not by guaranteeing the general manner of its transmission (as with the Vedas and the Pali Canon), but by furnishing historical particulars of the master-pupil lineage —names, biographies, dates, and circumstances of handing down the teaching.

T'ien-t'ai. The lineage of the T'ien-t'ai sect begins with Hui-ssŭ (515–576). He "went forth" when he was fifteen, and resolved at twenty that it was his vocation to save all mankind. He practiced asceticism and meditation, and attained the Dharma-Lotus samādhi, induced by weeks of alternately reciting and meditating on the *Lotus Sūtra.* After much fasting and meditation, he had a dream in which he sat in Maitreya's assembly on a giant lotus flower. He wept, thinking "In the Latter-day Dharma I have received the *Lotus Sūtra,* and now I have met Maitreya." This spurred him to even greater zeal, and many wondrous omens appeared.

The phrase "Latter-day Dharma" comes from the *Lotus Sūtra.* Indian texts distinguish three Dharma periods: (1) the True Dharma (0–500 A.N.), (2) the Counterfeit Dharma (501–1000 or 1500 A.N.), and (3) the Latter-day Dharma (10,000 years). Sixth-century Chinese put the Nirvāṇa at 949 B.C., so they thought that the Latter-day Period began about 550 A.D. Most of the great sectarian patriarchs adduced the advent of the Last Age as a reason why their teaching was necessary and timely. As preachers are always prone to do, they exploited the idea that the present age is sinful and degenerate in order to goad people into exertion. The *Lotus,* the *Diamond-Cutter,* and other Mahāyāna Sūtras say that people who uphold the True Dharma in the Last Time will earn immeasurable merit. Chinese and Japanese followers of the *Lotus Sūtra* correctly discerned the intent of such passages and often felt that they themselves were called to the career of Latter-day Saints.

To escape the dangers of war, Hui-ssŭ moved south to a mountain where he spent the rest of his life. The secluded mountain monastery had been institutionalized by famous monks of Eastern Chin (317–420), especially Hui-yüan. Such an environment favored study and meditation more than the busy metropolitan monasteries that enjoyed imperial favor through their proximity to the court. Most of the great sects started in the mountain temples and moved into the capital after achieving considerable success in the provinces. And most of the tsung lost their original purity and spiritual integrity amid the busyness and intrigue that accompanied fame and fortune. Schools that did not maintain a base in mountain monasteries perished when imperial disfavor, persecution, or internal degeneracy overtook them.

Chih-i (538–597), "the great master of T'ien-t'ai," became Hui-ssŭ's disciple, practiced Dharma-Lotus meditation, and attained samādhi when reading a passage in the *Lotus Sūtra* about a bodhisattva who burned his own body in a sandalwood fire as an offering to the Buddha. Later the master appointed him to lecture on the Prajñā Sūtra and the *Lotus,* and when he went south, turned the leadership of the Community over to Chih-i (who was then twenty-nine).

Chih-i and his followers spent the next eight years in Nanking, the capital of the Ch'en dynasty. Disgusted with the dissolute and turbulent life of the capital, he then withdrew to Mount T'ien-t'ai, in Chekiang, from which the T'ien-t'ai-tsung takes its name.

Chih-i laid equal emphasis on meditation and on doctrine study, on self-cultivation and propagating the teaching. Though he insisted that he was a plain practicer of meditation and not a philosopher, his doctrinal system is an architectonic marvel. It is a vast syncretism designed to comprise and harmonize all Buddhist doctrines. He accepted Hui-ssŭ's thesis that the *Lotus* rather than the *Nirvāṇa Sūtra* contains Śākyamuni's highest teaching, and that each of the other Sūtras speaks on several different levels because it is addressing a mixed audience. T'ien-t'ai distinguishes five periods in Śākyamuni's teaching career, four methods of teaching in Sūtras prior to the *Lotus* (sudden, gradual, secret indeterminate, and explicit indeterminate), and four modes of doctrine—the Tripiṭaka teaching (= Hīnayāna), the pervasive teaching (= Śūnyavāda), the special teaching (= Yogācāra), and the round/perfect teaching (= the *Lotus* doctrine).

As translations accumulated, Chinese scholars became puzzled over the discrepancies between the Sūtras. When the Śāstras contradicted each other, the Chinese had no trouble accepting that it was simply because at least one author was wrong; but the Sūtras were all supposed to be the word of the Buddha, who could not err and could not genuinely contradict himself. The Sūtras themselves furnished the rudiments of an explanation: the Buddha uses skillful means and preaches different doctrines to suit the conditions of his audience, and each Sūtra was delivered at a particular point in Śākyamuni's career.

The Community on Mount T'ien-t'ai prospered with patronage from the Sui imperial family for two decades after Chih-i's death, but declined under the T'ang, which did not appreciate the sect's close connections with the preceding dynasty. In the eighth century, T'ien-t'ai revived under the great master Chan-jan (711–781), who inspired some notable lay disciples to encompass Buddhism and Confucianism within one syncretic system. Out of this enterprise arose the Neo-Confucian school, which ironically became the most enduring and destructive of all Buddhism's enemies.

San-lun. The four Mādhyamika treatises translated by Kumārajīva were studied by a few scholars throughout the fifth century. Chih-i drew heavily on the fourth, the *Great Perfection of Wisdom Treatise,* for his early lectures on dhyāna, and composed a commentary to it. But for Chih-i, Mādhyamika was just one ingredient among many, and he had little relish for dialectic, which is the heart of Nāgārjuna's system.

Chi-tsang (549–623), the greatest master of the *San-lun* ("Three Treatise") school, rejected "classification of teachings" as a wrongheaded enterprise. Otherwise, the Three Treatise doctrine is quite simply a restatement of Nāgārjuna's teaching in a new vocabulary, with a few additional theses on matters such as the Two Truths where Nāgārjuna was too brief and vague.

The Three Treatise lineage died out after Chi-tsang. He was not a meditation master, and the Chinese were not prepared by their type of education to pursue enlightenment through the therapeutic exercise of dialectic.

Fa-hsiang. Yogācāra was introduced to China by Paramārtha (arrived in 546), whose most influential translation was that of Asanga's *Compendium of Mahāyāna.* A school grew up around this text, and it was perplexity about certain points in it that prompted Hsüan-tsang (596–664) to go to India and study. He spent fifteen months studying Vijñānavāda at Nālandā (see p. 45), went on a tour through South India, came back to Nālandā and studied some more, was accorded an audience and much honor by the Emperor Harṣa, and returned to China with a large collection of Sanskrit manuscripts. He spent the rest of his life translating the texts he had brought back and teaching Vijñānavāda to his pupils. His disciple K'uei-chi (632–682) is reckoned as the founder of the Fa-hsiang ("dharma-mark") school, which soon died out in China though it has survived in Japan, and was revived about 1908 by Yang Wen-hui, the father of the Chinese Buddhist revival.

Hua-yen. The Hua-yen sect was started by Tu-shun (557–640). As a boy he worked as a laborer in a military service batallion. At eighteen he went forth, and devoted himself to meditation, attaining miracle-working powers and becoming highly renowned. He concentrated on the *Avataṃsaka Sūtra* (*Hua-yen Ching*) just as Hui-ssŭ concentrated on the *Lotus Sūtra.* The third in line was Fa-tsang (643–712), the great architect of the school. In his young days he worked in Hsüan-tsang's translation bureau, and in his old age he assisted Śikṣānanda in the retranslation of the *Avataṃsaka.* He served as preceptor to four emperors, and wrote voluminously. Two eminent masters followed Fa-tsang: Ch'eng-kuan (738/737–838/820), and Tsung-mi (780–841). The sect did not survive the general suppression of Buddhism in 845.

The Hua-yen "classification of teachings" assigns top place to the *Avataṃsaka,* and the school's metaphysics centers on the concept of the Dharma-realm expounded in the Sūtra. The Dharma-realm has two aspects. As noumenon (*li*), it is the realm of suchness, of transcendental and immanent Dharma. As phenomenon (*shih*), it is the realm of the dharmas, the conditioned world of transmigration. The Hīnayānist sees the Dharma-realm of phenomena. Mādhyamika and Yogācāra, says Hua-yen, see the Dharma-realm of noumena. T'ien-t'ai and the *Awakening of Faith* (a Chinese

Yogācāra text falsely attributed to Aśvaghoṣa) are said to consider a Dharma-realm where phenomena and noumena do not impede each other. The Hua-yen teaching claims to see a Dharma-realm where phenomena do not impede each other but enter into each other and are identical with each other.

The Hua-yen doctrine is not so much a rational philosophy as a galaxy of concepts arrayed for contemplation. It is indeed sublime to look at, but it is not good for much else. This kind of intellectual yoga is a very hard road to samādhi, and in any place or time very few are ready for it.

T'ien-t'ai and Hua-yen succeeded better than *San-lun* ("Three Treatise") and Fa-hsiang because they were Chinese adaptations rather than Indian transplants. They did not engage much in formal arguments and proofs, for which the native Chinese tradition had little fondness. In China, gentlemen refrain from argument. Another strength of T'ien-t'ai and Hua-yen was that they gratified the endemic Chinese penchant for harmonizing things, that they assured unity in doctrine while permitting a full panoply of individual options. Since the third century B.C., Chinese thought has usually considered unity in ideas as a factor in sociopolitical unity, and has abhorred dissention in either realm.

The all-inclusiveness of T'ien-t'ai and Hua-yen diffused the energies of the individual and of the sects. Furthermore, they required a high degree of education and much book study. Starting from similar origins—mountain monks studying one Sūtra and meditating on it—there arose several popular sects during the sixth century, each of which radically simplified its statement of doctrine and advocated the exclusive and intense pursuit of some one practice. Some of these cults professed pessimism about the latter-day world, but they all fostered hope, enhanced faith in the efficacy of devout action, and released a torrent of religious energy. The two chief popular sects were the Ching-t'u-tsung ("Pure Land") and the Ch'an-tsung (Zen).

Pure Land. T'an-luan (476–542), the first master in the Pure Land lineage, got his religious vocation when, convalescing from a grave illness, he saw a vision of a heavenly gate opening to him. He decided to seek everlasting life, and sought it first in Taoism, which professed to have recipes for lengthening this life into an immortal one. Then he met the Indian Bodhiruci, who told him that Buddhism possessed a superior method of gaining everlasting life, and taught him the Amitābha texts. T'an-luan was convinced, burned his Taoist books, and concentrated on getting to the Pure (Happy) Land. He organized societies for recitation of Amitābha's name, and propagated the Pure Land cult with great success. He also laid the foundations of sectarian doctrine. He declared that even those who have committed evil deeds and atrocities are eligible for rebirth in the Western paradise if they sincerely desire it. But he maintained that those who revile the Dharma are excluded, for one thing because blasphemy is not conducive to aspiration, and for another, because the retribution for blasphemy is repeated rebirth in the lowest hell. T'an-luan asserted that even the merit a man seems to earn for himself is facilitated by the overarching power of Amita's vows, and that birth in the Pure Land and attainment of Buddhahood there are due to vow power. His stress on Other-power led him to advocate faith and recitation of Amitābha's name rather than meditation.

The next great Pure Land master was Tao-ch'o (562–645). He was born twenty years after T'an-luan's death, and as a young monk happened across T'an-luan's epitaph, the reading of which deeply affected him and turned his course to the Pure Land teaching. He was the first Pure Land master to stress latter-day pessimism. Like T'an-luan, he adopted the terms "easy path" and "path of the saints." He argued that in a degenerate age men did not have the capacity to follow the path of the saints, and that consequently they had no recourse except the Pure Land teaching.

The practice that Tao-ch'o proclaimed for ignorant people in the age of decay was *nien-fo,* which he interpreted not as "Buddha-contemplation" (the usual technical meaning of the term) but as "Buddha-invocation," calling the name of Amita. He asserted that reciting the Buddha's name with undistracted mind would overcome all evil, erase all sins, and assure rebirth in the Western paradise. His disciples engaged in recitation marathons, one monk setting the record of a million times in one week.

The Chinese Pure Land sect received its definitive shape at the hands of Tao-ch'o's great disciple Shan-tao (613–681). In doctrine, he denied two ideas then prevalent: (1) that the Happy Land is an inferior apparition-land where ordinary beings can attain rebirth, and (2) that the Happy Land is a superior and transcendental Buddha-field inaccessible to ordinary people. Shan-tao clarified his predecessors' ideas as to the means of attaining rebirth. He classified acts that lead to rebirth (in Sukhāvatī) as primary (*nien-fo*) and secondary (chanting Sūtras, meditating on the Buddha, worshipping Buddha-images, and singing praises to the Buddha). He insisted that both primary and secondary means should be practiced, and did so himself. It is said that he attained the Buddha-recollection samādhi.

Shan–tao was a zealous and skilled evangelist. He preached for over thirty years to monks and laymen in the capital, and convened big gatherings to chant "na-mo a-mi-t'o-fo" (salutation to Amita Buddha). He wrote out thousands of copies of the *Amita Sūtra* (*Smaller Sukhāvatī-vyūha*) and gave them to his innumerable disciples. He painted numerous pictures of the Pure Land and distributed them, causing the subject to become extremely popular in mid-T'ang painting. To promote singing Amita's praises, he wrote liturgical manuals. Famed for his tireless activity and his strict observance of the Vinaya, he was a holy eccentric. It is said that for more than thirty years he had no special sleeping place, did not take off his robes except to bathe, never raised his eyes to look at a woman, and gave no thought to fame or gain. When he recited the Buddha-name, a radiant splendor issued from his mouth. Legend says that in 681 he climbed the willow tree in front of his temple, jumped from it, and died. According to one view, he did this to get rid of his body and go to birth in Sukhāvatī. The Japanese Pure Land (*Jōdo*) schools consider that Shan-tao was an apparition-body of Amitābha. Shinran (see p. 103) says, "Shan-tao alone understood the Buddha's true intention."

The Amitābha cult was further promoted by Tz'u-min (680–748), who became converted to it while in India from 704 to 716. On returning to China he propagated the *nien-fo* practice among the common people, and vigorously denounced the Ch'an sect for practicing meditation to the exclusion of morality. He advocated the combined practice of meditation, scholarship, morality and Buddha-invocation. This is at variance with the exclusive nien-fo of Shan-tao, and a forerunner of the later syncretism between Pure Land and Ch'an.

The last great Pure Land master of T'ang times was Fa-chao (late eighth century), who advanced the cause of Amitism against competition from great masters of Ch'an, T'ien-t'ai, Chen-yen, and Hua-yen. He started out in T'ien-t'ai, and carried its syncretistic outlook over to his Pure Land doctrine. He was a noted composer of hymns. It is alleged that he received revelations from Amita and, through that Buddha's supervening power, performed miracles.

By the ninth century the Amita cult was so fully formed and so widely diffused that it ceased to need great masters. Only Ch'an withstood its influence. Yet by the sixteenth century Chinese Ch'an was permeated by Pure Land practices, and nowadays "na-mo a-mi-t'o fo" is chanted regularly in the daily liturgy of Ch'an monasteries.

The two chief Chinese departures from early Indian Amitābhist doctrine were reciting the name rather than meditating on the Buddha, and affirming that sinners, too, can go to the Pure Land. It has been noted that reciting sacred names was a popular practice in India, and it was certainly not a part of pre-Buddhist Chinese religion. T'an-luan's motive in explaining away the *Sukhāvatī-vyūha Sūtra's* statement that grave sinners are excluded from the effect of Amita's vow was the conviction that all living beings possess Buddha-nature. This idea originated in India, but it found such favor in China precisely because no native Chinese philosophy (except Moism, which became extinct before Buddhism was widely accepted in China) preached universal love and the worth of every man regardless of family or class.

During the eighth century, the Amita cult attracted emperors and slaves, scholars and women, artists and soldiers, monks and laymen. The common hope for rebirth in the Pure Land united the otherwise disparate segments of society. From the twelfth century, Neo-Confucian gentlemen disdained to share a cult that was both "vulgar" (since the common people had it) and "foreign"; but their wives continued to recite "na-mo a-mi-t'o fo," and mandarin boys as they grew up had to expunge the devotion learned from their mothers. No native Chinese god has ever commanded the universal worship that Amitābha has received.

Ch'an. Meditation texts were among the earliest translations, because lay disciples of An Shih-kao were practicing dhyāna and needed manuals. Their purpose was to get the superknowledges, especially the mundane ones; and if we are to credit the tales in their biographies, some of them succeeded. Lao-tzu and Chuang-tzu mention various yogic techniques, and popular Han Taoism developed and enriched the repertory, so that Buddhist dhyāna found a well-oriented clientele.

Most of the early missionaries and eminent Chinese monks were proficient in meditation. The *Lives of Eminent Monks,* completed about 530 A.D., contains biographies of twenty meditators and twenty-one wonder-workers, besides the translators and commentators who were also noted for dhyāna. So it is clear that Indian methods of dhyāna were effective and popular in China. Nevertheless, meditation was just one practice among many in the large monasteries and the famous sects of the late sixth century. The student was involved in lectures and reading, rituals, and sundry pious works to such an extent that he had little time and insufficient encouragement to practice contemplation.

The Ch'an sect arose to meet the demand for a well-grounded and lasting tradition specializing in meditation. It began, like the other Chinese sects, as a lineage of masters devoted to one text, in this case the *Laṅkāvatāra Sūtra.* Its early history is obscured by legends figmented in the eighth century and later. It seems a fact that Bodhidharma, an Indian dhyāna master and champion of the *Laṅkāvatāra,* arrived by sea in Canton about 470, stayed briefly in South China, then went north and stayed there until about 520. Legend says that while in the South Bodhidharma met the pious Emperor Wu of Liang, who asked him: "Have I earned merit by my lifelong temple building, donation, and worship offerings?" Bodhidharma said: "No merit at all." The emperor, disappointed, banished Bodhidharma. The tale is anachronistic, as Bodhidharma was already in the North by 483, and Wu did not become emperor until 502. The story, though, points up a cardinal idea of Ch'an, that true merit is not that which stems from good works and leads to mundane good luck, but that which springs from insight into the Dharmakāya, which is one's own true nature. This is the distinction between finite or relative and infinite or absolute merit that is made repeatedly in the Śūnyavādin Sūtras.

Bodhidharma settled in a mountain temple near Lo-yang, where he acquired at least two disciples and taught them the *Laṅkāvatāra.* Legend says that in this monastery he spent nine years gazing at a wall, that he sat continuously until his legs fell off, and that he cut off his eyelids so that his gaze would never falter. The term "wall gazing" occurs in an early pamphlet attributed to Bodhidharma, and the earliest biography says that he taught "wall contemplation." This was probably a kind of "formless meditation" like that recommended in *The Awakening of Faith,* and the Japanese *shikantaza* ("just sitting") practice.

Bodily mutilation is a frequent theme in Ch'an legends. It serves several purposes: by example to encourage intrepid striving, to counteract ordinary timidity, and to arouse energy by fixing the imagination on intense physical pain. It is a manneristic exaggeration of the common Buddhist meditation on suffering.

The Second Patriarch in the *Laṅkāvatāra* lineage and the Ch'an sect is Hui-k'o (487–593). In youth he studied Taoism, the classics, and Buddhist doctrine. When a mature man, he met Bodhidharma and studied with him for six (or nine) years, at the end of which Bodhidharma designated him his successor. Hui-k'o led a wandering life after his master's death, was persecuted by hostile monks, and hid in the mountains during the persecution of 574. After the restoration of Buddhism, he returned to the capital and lived out his old age in peace.

A fragment of Hui-k'o's doctrine has been preserved in *The Lives of Further Eminent Monks*. It expresses succinctly the fundamental Ch'an teaching:

> The deep principle of the True is utterly non-different. From of old, one is confused about the Gem and thinks it is a piece of tile. When suddenly oneself wakes up, there is the real jewel. Ignorance and wisdom are the same and without difference. Know that the myriad things are all identical with suchness. When you regard the body and do not distinguish it from the Buddha, why go on to seek [nirvāṇa] without remainder?

All these ideas we have seen in Indian Śūnyavāda and Vajrayāna—the identity of saṃsāra and nirvāṇa, the tathāgata-garbha as the gem of intrinsic Buddhahood, this body as the Buddha-body, and the futility of seeking for nirvāṇa as if it were another thing among things. The Ch'an masters, like the Tantric poets, did not invent new concepts but extracted the most powerful religious ideas from a diffuse literature and presented them in concentrated, punchy form.

The Third Patriarch, Seng-ts'an (died 606) is relatively unknown. He was an intelligent boy, and grew up to become one of Hui-k'o's disciples. He studied with him for six years, received the Dharma-seal from him, and fled along with him to the mountains in the persecution of 574. Seng-ts'an is credited with authorship of a long poem, *The Inscription on Faith in Mind,* which has remained immensely popular to this day.

The Fourth Patriarch, Tao-hsin (580–651), went forth when he was seven, studied six years with another teacher, and then came to Seng-ts'an and stayed with him for eight or nine years. He was famed as a thaumaturgist. When he visited a city besieged by bandits, the dry springs flowed with water, and the bandits dispersed when he chanted the Prajñā Sūtras. In 624 he took up residence on a mountain in Hupeh and stayed there the rest of his life. It is said that he foresaw his imminent death, that he died to the accompaniment of natural prodigies, and that three years after death his body was incorrupt. He had a number of disciples.

The Fifth Patriarch, Hung-jen (601–674), went forth as a child, was soon recognized for his talent by Tao-hsin, and spent the whole night in meditation and attained enlightenment without reading the Sūtras. The *Platform Sūtra* gives a vivid glimpse of Hung-jen's community, said to number over a thousand disciples, in Huang-mei county, Hupeh, on East Mountain, so called because it lies to the east of the Fourth Patriarch's mountain. Not much is known about his teaching, but he seems to have drawn on the *Avataṃsaka* and the Prajñā Sūtras, as well as the *Laṅkāvatāra*; and the *Platform Sūtra* may be right in stating that Hung-jen especially encouraged his followers to recite the *Diamond-Cutter.*

That the Ch'an movement was growing and not just perpetuating itself in the seventh century is indicated by the branching of successions. Tao-hsin had two eminent disciples, Hung-jen (601–674) and Fa-yung (594–657). Fa-yung's branch prospered and survived at least until the eighth generation; it was taken to Japan about 800. Hung-jen, the Fifth Patriarch, had eleven notable disciples, of whom the most important were Shen-hsiu (606–706) and Hui-neng (638–713).

Shen-hsiu was the chief of Hung-jen's Community when the boy Hui-neng arrived to seek admission, and he was widely recognized as the Sixth Patriarch. His branch, later called Northern Ch'an, became very popular in Lo-yang and received imperial recognition.

Hui-neng was, like many other great Dharma-masters, the son of a gentry family that had fallen on hard times. His father was demoted from office and banished to Kwangtung where he soon died. Hui-neng sold firewood to help support his widowed mother. One day he chanced to hear a man reciting the *Diamond-Cutter*. He experienced an awakening, and asked the reciter where he came from. The man referred him to Hung-jen, so the boy took leave of his mother and went to call on the Fifth Patriarch, who said: "If you're from Kwangtung, you're a barbarian. How can you become a Buddha?" Hui-neng answered, "There is no north and south in Buddha-nature. Although my barbarian's body and your body are not the same, what difference is there in our Buddha-nature?" Hung-jen sent the bright boy to work as a lay brother, pounding rice in the mill.

The *Platform Sūtra* tells a suspect tale of how Hui-neng received the Dharma-succession from Hung-jen. After the boy had been working in the mill for eight months, the Patriarch ordered his disciples each to exercise their insight and write a stanza, and announced that he would give his robe, Dharma, and succession to anyone who revealed enlightenment. Shen-hsiu wrote his verse secretly on a wall at midnight:

> The body is the Bodhi Tree,
> The mind is like a bright mirror-and-stand.
> At all times wipe it dilligently,
> Don't let there be any dust.

The Fifth Patriarch, say the partisans of Hui-neng, told Shen-hsiu privately that he had arrived at the front gate but had not entered it, and sent him away crestfallen to try again. Hui-neng heard a boy reciting Shen-hsiu's verse, composed his own reply, and had someone write it up on another wall:

> Bodhi really has no tree;
> The bright mirror also has no stand.
> Buddha-nature is forever pure; (or: Really no
> thing exists)
> Where is there room for dust?

The Fifth Patriarch, so the story goes, said in front of the crowd that the verse showed incomplete understanding, but summoned Hui-neng at midnight and expounded the *Diamond-Cutter* to him. Hearing it once, Hui-neng awakened right away, and received the Dharma and the robe without anyone else's knowing it. The master then ordered his disciple to go away immediately lest jealous people harm him.

This story shows several distinctive features of early Ch'an. The Chinese character *wu* (read *satori* in Japanese) means to awaken, to understand. It translates Sanskrit *budh,* the root of *Buddha* and *bodhi.* In Ch'an it signifies an opening of insight, a change to a higher level of understanding similar to the "recognition" that Kauṇḍinya experienced when he heard the First Sermon and to what the audience in a Mahāyāna Sūtra experiences upon hearing a Dharma-discourse. Hui-neng had his two awakenings upon hearing the *Diamond-Cutter*. This is in accord with the general Indian notion that hearing is the proximate cause of attaining insight. It also shows that early Ch'an acknowledged degrees of awakening and a progression from lower to higher. Hung-jen's question and Hui-neng's answer show that the school took seriously the Buddha-nature of all beings, and sought supreme, perfect enlightenment in this life.

Shen-hsiu's verse expresses the Ch'an tenet that this very body is the Buddha. "Mirror-knowledge" is a synonym for enlightenment in Pali and Sanskrit texts, and the mirror is a widespread symbol for the psyche. The Ch'an meditator, like every other meditator, continually wipes away distractions, random and meandering thoughts, until finally no more dust alights on his mirror. Hui-neng's verse plays one-upmanship by switching to the absolute standpoint, a familiar gambit in Śūnyavādin Sūtras. It does not refute Shen-hsiu, but, by the conventions of the game, Hui-neng is one up.

That the crowd was covetous of the Dharma and prepared to do bodily harm to someone in order to get it, must have seemed thoroughly plausible to eighth-century readers. Vicious intrigues within the Saṅgha are well attested for this period. The rivalries between Shen-hsiu's and Hui-neng's branches were prosecuted with slander, fabrication, competition for official favor, and political machinations to get rivals banished or dispossessed.

Hui-neng is represented by his later school as an untutored genius, illiterate and unschooled in the scriptures. The myth serves a purpose: the school opposed book-scholars' pretensions and called laymen and uneducated people to attain awakening simply by using their native talent. The *Platform Sūtra* shows Hui-neng as illiterate, which may be less than true; but it also shows him quoting the Sūtras, handling a large technical vocabulary, and giving sermons that, though not high prose by T'ang standards, are far from uncultivated.

The private interview with the master has remained a crucial part of Ch'an procedure ever since. Dialogs that occurred in these encounters form a substantial part of later Ch'an literature. They are terse, often witty, sometimes bizarre and obscure. The master usually had a lot of students, and only two or three short periods a day were set aside for interviews, so the chance was precious. In addition, the student's hopes and fears were usually keyed up by long waiting and intense striving, so that the meeting had the sudden-death quality of a duel. The master diagnoses the student's problem and treats it. Sometimes he simply explains or advises. Sometimes he provokes, shocks, or otherwise manipulates the student. The Ch'an strategy is to catch a person at the critical moment and do the appropriate thing that triggers awakening. The Buddho-Taoists, amalgamating the general Indian doctrine that the Buddha adapts his teaching to his hearers' capacity and the Taoist ideal of going with the grain of the Tao, had said repeatedly that the Holy Man accords with things, teaches according to the critical situation, responds to appeals. Ch'an follows Taoism in recognizing the uniqueness of each natural specimen. No two trees, rocks, tigers, or men are really the same. Chinese law, unlike Hellenistic and European law, was a respecter of persons, and never maintained that what is fair for one is fair for all. Ch'an masters similarly treat each case as *sui generis,* acting and expecting responses with spontaneity and without preconceptions or premeditation.

Hui-neng's first sermon (as given in the *Platform Sūtra*) deals with the relation between wisdom and meditation. He says that they are not two things but one. Meditation is the substance of wisdom, and wisdom is the function of meditation, just as the lamp is the substance (*t'i,* "body") of light and light is the function of the lamp. The "one-course samādhi" is coursing in a sincere mind at all times, whether walking, standing, sitting, or lying. As the *Vimalakīrti* says, "A sincere mind is the bodhi-ground. A sincere mind is the Pure Land." In other words, meditation is having an earnest and concentrated mind. It is to be carried out in all postures and is to suffuse all one's activities.

Hui-neng was said to have received the Dharma from Hung-jen in 661. He went south again and stayed in hiding. One day in 676 he showed up at a monastery in Canton where the master Yin-tsung was lecturing on the *Nirvāṇa Sūtra.* He attracted the attention of the master and delighted him, says the story, with a profound discussion of the *Nirvāṇa Sūtra,* whereupon the master first conferred ordination on Hui-neng (who had been a layman until then), and then became his disciple. In the spring of the next year, Hui-neng went to Mount Ts'ao-ch'i (in Kwangtung), where he is said to have delivered as an inaugural address the first sermon in the *Platform Sūtra,* and where he spent the rest of his life, acquiring several thousand disciples, including both monks and laymen. He announced his approaching death to his disciples a month before it happened. It is said that, for two days after his coffin was interred on Mount Ts'ao-ch'i, a bright light arose from it up into the sky.

After Hui-neng's death, his school remained in obscurity for two decades, while Shen-hsiu's school enjoyed popularity in Ch'ang-an and Lo-yang. Then in 732 Hui-neng's disciple Shen-hui organized a big conference in which he launched an attack on Shen-hsiu's successor, asserting that Hui-neng was the true Sixth Patriarch. In 745 he was appointed to a temple in Lo-yang from which he prosecuted his campaign against the rival school and enjoyed brilliant success as a preacher. After eight years, a powerful official who favored Northern Ch'an accused Shen-hui of sedition, and the emperor banished him. But after the rebel An Lu-shan drove the emperor into exile in 756, Shen-hui was called back and put in charge of an ordination platform amid the ruins of Lo-yang, where he performed ordinations and earned money, through the sale of monk certificates, for the loyalist war effort.

Shen-hui was considered the Seventh Patriarch by his followers, but other houses in the Hui-neng line gave him no special honor.

The acrimony and the threats and charges of violence that marked the dispute over the patriarchal succession seem as sordid as the mutual calumnies and assaults of Lenin and his left-wing confreres, and sprang from similar causes. The Ch'an people were in life-and-death earnest. They had forsaken the comfortable dilletantism of the all-embracing sects such as T'ien-t'ai. They wasted no time on "classifying teachings," on arranging pretty smorgasbords of doctrine. The roots of the movement were in the back-country mountain temples where life was rough and rigorous, where isolation and exclusive concentration on one quest tended to foster extremism. The Ch'an movement, too, was undoubtedly inebriated by its successes, by its ability to lead the seeker to enlightenment in this life, by the presence of men who were virtual Buddhas, and by the way that earnest people from all classes of society rallied to the Ch'an teachers. Like the builders of other popular Chinese sects, they were convinced that the robe of destiny had devolved on them, and this seemed to justify drastic expedients, as well as to render purity of teaching extraordinarily momentous.

In 796, the emperor called a council to decide the true Ch'an teaching and to settle the controversy about the lineages. Afterward an imperial decree designated Shen-hui "Seventh Patriarch," thus confirming that Hui-neng, not Shen-hsiu, was the Sixth. Posthumous imperial honors were conferred on Hui-neng, and the controversy was over.

The characteristics of early Ch'an are well shown in the interviews with Hui-neng related in the *Platform Sūtra.* A monk named Fa-ta ("Dharma Penetration") had been reciting the *Lotus Sūtra* for years, but was confused and in doubt about what the Sūtra meant. He went and called on Hui-neng, who asked him to recite the text and then interpreted it for him, telling him, "Listen to the one Buddha-vehicle and do not seek the Two Vehicles. . . . If you awaken to this Dharma, in one instant your mind will open, and you will become prominent in the world." In other words, the One Vehicle is the Sudden Teaching. The master then said that if your mind is right, you recite the *Lotus,* but if your mind is wrong, the *Lotus* recites you. When Fa-ta heard this, he had a great awakening and broke into tears. From that day, he understood the profound meaning of the *Sūtra,* and continued to recite it.

One of the basic features of Ch'an is "not setting up the written word as an authority." Otherwise phrased, it is "not clinging to written words and not separating from written words." Hui-neng had no objection to recitation of the scriptures; he owed his own first awakening to an itinerant Sūtra-chanter. But he disparaged the all-too-common practice of mere reading without comprehension: "If you cling staunchly to your recitation and regard it as an achievement, you do not differ from a yak that loves its tail." Real and efficacious practice is illumined by prajñā.

Hui-neng's explanation of the *Lotus* is straightforward and intelligible, like most early Ch'an teaching and unlike the sayings of many later masters. He regularly contrasts the conventional meaning of a doctrine with its "true" or absolute meaning. This is a frequent device in the Śūnyavādin Sūtras. Its purpose is not to contradict conventional truths on their own level, but to jolt the hearer right out of the habitual and conventional. Fa-ta's failure to understand the central idea of the *Lotus* was probably due to lack of education. Many novices in China were trained simply to recite one Sūtra, which they learned by rote and without explanation. Often it was the only book that they had read or could read. They made their living reciting it in the streets, or at funeral and memorial rites. Hui-neng and Shen-hui expounded the Prajñā teachings to monks and laymen who had known only the religion of merit, who had been blindly performing pious acts without knowing their meaning and purpose. No wonder that men like Fa-ta broke into tears of amazement and gratitude.

The awakening that climaxes the Ch'an interview tale is triggered by the master's words, but usually seems much stronger than the mere words would warrant. This is equally so with Śākyamuni's first sermon and Kauṇḍinya's awakening (see p. 26). One factor is the spiritual aura, the charisma, of the master. Ch'an is said to be "a special transmission outside doctrines," a direct transmission from mind to mind. Another factor is that the master's instruction was directed to the specific condition of the inquirer, which the ordinary reader is unlikely to duplicate. Ch'an is for those with keen faculties, and the teaching is given only to those who are ripe for it. A third factor is the interaction between master and disciple. The tense, expectant inquirer feels strongly that he is in the presence of a wise man who can read his character and prescribe for him. He is relieved and thankful to have someone concentrate on him, know him as he really is, and "point directly at his nature." And the student is humiliated, disappointed, and stimulated to greater effort when the master candidly criticizes him.

The early Ch'an contemplative exercise was simply striving constantly to have no notions, and to see one's nature and become a Buddha. It meant playing a simple, difficult, and fascinating game of cat-and-mouse with one's "fundamental mind." Interviews with the master were a crucial adjunct. As generations passed, sayings and dialogs of the old masters were collected and came to be used as themes for contemplation. The "old case" or "public document" (*kung-an,* Japanese *kōan*) literature and exercise were fully developed by the early twelfth century. Though kung-an meditation is especially associated with the Lin-chi (Japanese Rinzai) subsect, it is also practiced by the other branches.

Huai-jang's greatest disciple was Tao-i (707–786), also called Ma-tsu. Born in Szechuan, he went forth under a local Ch'an master, then went to Huai-jang at Mount Nan-yüeh in Kiangsi. One day Ma-tsu was sitting in meditation, and Huai-jang asked, "What are you doing?"

"I wish to become a Buddha."

The master picked up a tile and began grinding it with a stone.

"What are you doing?"

"I am polishing this tile to make a mirror."

"But no amount of polishing will ever make a mirror out of a brick."

"And no amount of sitting cross-legged will ever make a Buddha out of you."

"What am I to do then?"

"It is like driving a cart. When it doesn't move, do you whip the cart or the ox? Are you sitting cross-legged to practice meditation, or to become a Buddha? If it is to practice meditation, that does not consist of sitting or lying down. If it is to become a Buddha, the Buddha has no fixed form. You cannot take hold of him or let him go. To think that you can obtain Buddhahood by sitting is simply to kill the Buddha, and until you give up the idea that you can so obtain it, you won't come near the truth."

Ma-tsu became Huai-jang's Dharma-heir, traveled around for a while, then settled and taught at a temple of his own in Kiangsi. His appearance inspired amazement and awe: "He strode along like a bull and glared about him like a tiger. If he stretched out his tongue, it reached up over his nose; on the soles of his feet were imprinted two circular marks." He used shouts and blows to shock the student into awakening.

Ma-tsu's chief successor, Huai-hai of Mount Pai-chang (749–814), created a new Vinaya and gave Ch'an community life its classic and distinctive form. The chief innovation in his rule is the requirement that all monks do manual labor: "One day no work, one day no food." Other Buddhist monasteries owned much land which was tilled by serfs. The Ch'an monks had taken to manual labor to support themselves as early as the Fourth Patriarch. Pai-chang made labor mandatory. The T'ang Ch'an masters acquired considerable tracts of mountain and waste land, and developed them by means of work parties of monks. They grew rice, cut bamboo, and developed tea plantations. These enterprises made the monks less dependent on donors and their whims, and obviated the charge that they were parasites on society. But physical work also served as an integral part of the spiritual discipline. The exercise counteracted the lethargy and depression that can come from sitting in meditation. Also, hoeing the fields and picking tea leaves were performed mindfully as part of day-and-night meditation.

When Pai-chang was old and feeble, his monks took his garden tools away from him, but he refused to eat until they let him go out and work again.

The most decisive catastrophe in the history of Chinese Buddhism was the proscription of 845. The external causes were rivalry between the Buddhists and the Taoists, and factional strife at the imperial court between the administrators on the one hand and the eunuchs on the other. In addition, the Saṅgha had accumulated a disproportionate share of the nation's wealth, had taken out of use large quantities of bronze and iron to make images, and had acquired tax-exempt status for some 260,000 clerics, 100,000 temple serfs, and a host of lay employes. Taoists' malice and bureaucratic concern for the national economy sufficed to persuade the emperor, who in 841 ordered that clerics who practiced magic, kept women, or otherwise violated the discipline should be laicized, and that money and real estate owned by monks or nuns should be confiscated by the government. This is no more than a devout Buddhist monarch would do to purify the Saṅgha. But in 845, the emperor first ordered a census of the clergy and its property, and then decreed the destruction of all except a few designated temples, confiscation and melting down of metal objects, returning the monks and nuns to lay life, and confiscation of the Saṅgha's lands and serfs. This proscription, unlike the previous ones, was effective throughout all of China. But the emperor died in 846, probably poisoned by the longevity pills his Taoist mentors had been feeding him. The new emperor started by executing the Taoist leaders who had instigated the persecution, and soon gave permission for the restitution of Buddhism.

Many sects perished entirely during this short, severe persecution. Only Ch'an prospered after the restoration. It had suffered like the other sects, but survived because it was less dependent on libraries, images, and the pomp and circumstance of temple cult. Even so, the metropolitan line of Shen-hui died out, and subsequent growth came in the lines of Southern mountain masters.

One of Pai-chang's successors was Ling-yu of Kuei-shan (771–853). When twenty-three he came to Pai-chang, who recognized his talent and took him as an attendant. One day the master said, "Who's there?"

"It's Ling-yu."

"Poke and see if there's still some fire in the stove."

Ling-yu poked around, and said, "There's no fire."

Pai-chang got up, went to the stove, poked quite a bit, managed to stir up a small glow, and said to his pupil, "Isn't this fire?" Ling-yu was awakened, knelt down, and bowed in gratitude to the master.

This *kung-an* (*kōan*) is readily intelligible. Fire stands for Buddha-nature. The disciple had not found his "nature" because he had not searched hard enough. Pai-chang commented to Ling-yu that seeing Buddha-nature depends on the right moment, the cause (the student's inherent Buddhahood), and the accessory cause (the master's direct pointing at the mind). The beauty of kung-an language is that it coins its vocabulary freshly and impromptu, avoiding scholastic terminology and using natural symbols. But the kung-an is mastered not when the symbols are identified with technical terms but when, for example, Buddha-nature is experienced as directly as the glowing coals.

Ch'an has been accused of iconoclasm and antinomianiam. In the eighth century, a lay follower of T'ien-t'ai charged that "those who travel the Ch'an path go so far as to teach the people that there is neither Buddha nor Dharma and that neither sin nor goodness has any significance." He alleged that ordinary people took this as license to sin, and were drawn to destruction like moths to a candle. Then there is the tale of T'ien-jan (died 824) who on a cold night took down the wooden Buddha-image in the shrine hall and made a fire with it. When he was accused of sacrilege, he said, "I was only looking for a Buddha-relic." "How can you expect to find a relic in a piece of wood?" "Well then, I am only burning a piece of wood, after all."

It may well be that some people took Ch'an teachings as an excuse to sin, just as some have so taken the Pure Land and Christian teachings that sinners may attain paradise. But the Ch'an masters required strict discipline from their clerical followers and sound morality from lay disciples. T'ien-jan's burning the image was indeed an act of sacrilege, and his companions' reaction is sufficient proof that Ch'an at that time did not condone the destruction of sacred objects. He got away with it, and it was reported, because he gave his act a transcendental significance and handled the repartee with wit.

Ch'an has kept the monastic system and has not discarded rituals, images, or the pantheon. Its style and language are distinctively Chinese, but its essence is the core teaching of Indian Mahāyāna. In some ways, too, Ch'an runs counter to major Chinese values. The Chinese as a whole have always loved magic, but the lives of the Ch'an masters contain very few references to the magic powers the dhyāna expert is supposed to attain. Confucian gentleman and Taoist adept both consider themselves above manual labor, but Ch'an trainees and masters toil like coolies. The glory of the Ch'an-tsung is not that it made Buddhism thoroughly Chinese, but that it extracted, concentrated, and made efficacious the essence of the Dharma.

From Sung to the Present. The story of Chinese Buddhism from 900 to 1900 is one of a golden later summer (900–1300), an Indian summer in the fifteenth century under the early Ming, and a fall shading into winter thereafter. No generation was without eminent monks, and yet the place of Buddhism in national life declined under government restrictions on entrance to the monastic orders, curtailments of monasteries' activities, and relentless anti-Buddhist propaganda from the Neo-Confucians who controlled the education system and the imperial examinations.

A modest revival began in the late nineteenth century, stimulated initially by the need to rebuild monasteries and reprint scriptures destroyed in Central China during the T'ai-p'ing rebellion (1850–1864). The rebels, who fervently professed a kind of Christianity, looted and burned most of the great monasteries in the areas they occupied. The shock stimulated both monks and laymen. Soon scripture-printing societies and study clubs were active. Some young monks who acquired modern ideas through lay-initiated schools became revolutionaries and participated in the overthrow of the Manchu dynasty in 1911. However, these radicals were not approved by the majority of the Saṅgha, who considered that a monk should stay out of politics and that he should study the scriptures rather than modern secular subjects.

The most famous of these radicals was the modernist monk T'ai-hsü (1890–1947). He was never accepted by the abbots of the great Ch'an monasteries of Central and South China, who held the real power in the Saṅgha, and who were carrying out extensive revitalization of their institutions along traditional lines. But he set up schools, introduced Western-style classroom instruction, taught secular subjects and foreign languages including Tibetan and Pali, and revived the study of the scholastic treatises, especially of the Fa-hsiang school. T'ai-hsü and his followers opened up relations with coreligionists abroad, and promoted the idea of a world fellowship of Buddhists. They announced an ambitious program of education, preaching, welfare, and economic development work, and attempted to implement it insofar as their resources and the troubled state of the country allowed.

The Nationalist regime in Mainland China fluctuated between mild hostility and mild support for Buddhism, but by and large allowed proponents of the Dharma a freedom they had not had during two and half centuries of Manchu rule, when all private associations were under suspicion of treason. When the Communists took over the Mainland in 1949, they were committed to wiping out all religion as soon as it could be done expediently. First, they declared that the clergy were parasites on society. Then in 1951 they confiscated the land holdings of the monasteries and so deprived the monks and nuns of the means to carry on religious activities. Young monks and nuns were returned to lay status, and the older clerics were put to work farming, weaving, running vegetarian restaurants, or teaching school. They were subjected to brainwashing to cleanse their minds of non-Marxist ideas. Then in 1953, a Chinese Buddhist Association was organized, so that the government could supervise and manipulate the still sizable Buddhist community, and so that China could reap the diplomatic advantages of representation at international Buddhist gatherings. Famous and beautiful old temples were maintained at government expense, Buddhist art works were safeguarded, and sites such as the Yünkang caves were designated national treasures. Then when the Great Cultural Revolution got under way, Red Guards proceeded to destroy Buddhist buildings and monuments along with other reminders of China's past. It is reported that by 1966 all Buddhist activities on the Mainland had been stopped.

In 1930 there were said to be 738,000 monks and nuns and 267,000 Buddhist temples in China. This was by far the largest clergy in China, or in any national church in the world. The majority did not live in strictly run monasteries, but at least 50,000 did. There was much idleness and laxity, but also much diligence and rigor. Buddhism was not a prominent force in national life, but insofar as Republican China was religious, it was more Buddhist than anything else.

Many monks have fled from Communist China to Hong Kong and Taiwan, where Buddhist associations operate freely and show a certain amount of vitality. In addition, Buddhism has some following among expatriate Chinese communities in Malaysia, Singapore, the Philippines, Vietnam, and San Francisco.

Japan

The Buddhism of Korea and Vietnam is Chinese in origin, sects, doctrines, and institutions. To this day, Korean and Vietnamese monks read the scriptures in Chinese. The religion has taken on a pronounced national coloring in each of these countries, and has played an interesting part in their histories, but has departed from Chinese models no more than Hungarian Presbyterianism and American Lutheranism have deviated from the original churches of Calvin and Luther.

Japanese Buddhism, too, uses Chinese as its canonical language, drew its models and inspiration from China, and is divided into sects that either originated in China or derive from Chinese sects. Nevertheless, its institutions and social character differ as much from those of Chinese Buddhism as Japanese society differs from Chinese.

Between 550 and 600, various Korean kings sent Buddha-images and Sūtras to the Japanese imperial court. Some Korean monks were resident in Japan, and the first Japanese nuns and monks were ordained. The first Korean gifts were accompanied by a memorial extolling Buddhism as productive of merit and wisdom. The Japanese got the idea that worshipping these foreign deities would bring good luck to the nation, and at first judged the new religion entirely on short-range consequences; when a plague broke out, the Buddha-image was dumped into a moat, and the first temple was razed. When another plague broke out later, images were again thrown into the moat and the nuns were defrocked. When the plague still did not stop, the emperor agreed to permit Buddhist cult freely.

Japan was in process of consolidating a centralized monarchy out of a federation of tribes when Buddhism arrived, bearing the high culture of China and motivated to convert and civilize. Confucians did not like to go abroad and teach among "barbarians," so in Japan the Buddhists had the field to themselves for centuries. It was desire for mundane fortune and cultural prestige that made the Japanese hospitable to the Dharma, and from the first it was accepted that religion is primarily an organ of national life, and only secondarily a ministration to the individual's needs.

During the seventh century, under a series of devout emperors, Buddhism was developed as part of the state apparatus. Temples were founded, monks were ordained, and public ceremonies were sponsored for the well-being of the nation. Four Chinese sectarian systems were imported. In 625, a Korean who had studied under Chi-tsang introduced the study of the San-lun (Japanese Sanron) and of the Hīnayāna Ch'eng-shih (Jōjitsu) treatise. In 658, two Japanese monks who had studied under Hsüan-tsang introduced the study of Vasubandhu's *Abhidharma-kośa* (*Kusha*). A Japanese monk went to China in 653, studied the Fa-hsiang (Hossō) teaching under Hsüan-tsang for over ten years, then returned and introduced it to Japan. Other Koreans and other foreign-returned Japanese reinforced the initial transmissions. Kusha, Jōjitsu, and Sanron were never more than curriculum subjects, but Hossō became a wealthy ecclesiastical corporation and has maintained an institutional existence to the present day. In 1948, it had about eighty temples and a thousand clerics. These scholastic treatises must have puzzled early Japanese students, whom we can imagine reading them with the same attitude of knowledge-is-good-for-you-especially-if-it-hurts with which their modern compatriots often tackle Hegel, Heidegger, and Tillich.

In the eighth century, when the capital was fixed at Nara, the Hua-yen (Kegon) sect was introduced by several teachers—Korean, Chinese, and Indian—and rapidly acquired great influence. The Hua-yen world view was adapted to political ideology by equating Vairocana with the emperor and the fourth Dharma-realm, that of phenomena not impeding each other, with Japanese society. The implicit metaphor of the spider and his web fits to perfection the society that the Japanese have created over the intervening centuries, and a study of Kegon renders more intelligible the peculiar Japanese blend of individualism and collectivism. Abstract philosophy was beyond the grasp of Nara intellectuals, but Kegon presented a concrete world vision giving spiritual elevation and political orientation.

In 752, a collosal bronze image of Vairocana was dedicated at the Tōdaiji (Eastern Great Temple) in Nara, where two years later the Chinese Vinaya master Ganjin established an ordination center. The Japanese government permitted ordinations only at approved centers, which were kept few, and so it maintained some control over the Saṅgha. This system, though, gave certain sects a monopoly, enhanced their power, and led to the typically feudal sectarian structure in which branch temples are ritually dependent on one head temple, which in turn is sometimes economically dependent on its client temples. The Great Buddha is still in Nara, but his network has been small for many centuries. The Kegon sect now counts about 125 temples and 500 clerics.

Buddhism strongly influenced Japanese social customs and material culture during the Nara period. Arts and crafts—architecture, sculpture, painting, carpentry, metal casting, calligraphy, and papermaking—were stimulated to bigger and better production by the demand for cult articles. Artisans were brought from China and Korea, and Japanese craftsmen were trained. Monks also introduced the Chinese mundane sciences: calendar-making, astronomy, geomancy, and magic. Buddhist ritual permeated court observances. The public bath and cremation, two of the most notable features of Japanese life, were introduced under Buddhist influence at this time. Monks served as scribes and clerks, providing the literate skills necessary for the Chinese-style administration that the imperial regime was trying to institute. They also acted as engineers in building roads, bridges, dikes, and irrigation systems. Wandering monks explored distant parts of the country, and drew the first Japanese maps.

During this period, the imperial authority was virtually the only large entrepreneur in the country, which did not yet have either an independent landed aristocracy or a sizable merchant community. As part of the colonization process, the emperor ordered each province to build a seven-storied pagoda, a monastery for twenty monks, and a convent for ten nuns. Copies of the *Golden Radiance Sūtra* were distributed to each province. The monks and court officials who could understand the scriptures in Chinese were a tiny elite. The copying and distribution of Sūtras did much to spread a knowledge of Chinese, even though the immediate aim was to create talismans rather than to acquire knowledge.

The capital was moved to Heian (Kyōto) in 794 in order to rusticate the corrupt and politically meddlesome Nara sects. Six years earlier, in 788, a young monk named Saichō (767–822) had built a little temple on Mount Hiei, northeast of Kyōto. He soon received the patronage of the emperor, who sent him in 804 to study in China. During his year there, he studied T'ien-t'ai (Japanese Tendai) and on returning to Japan he propagated this teaching and so founded a new sect. He kept his monks in seclusion on Mount Hiei while they underwent a twelve-year period of study and meditation. Some of his graduates stayed on the mountain, while others left to serve the state as scribes, engineers, and teachers. Saichō tried hard to get an ordination center established on Mount Hiei; but, due to the opposition of the Nara clerics, the center was only authorized in 827, five years after Saichō's death. He received the posthumous title Dengyō Daishi ("Great Master Who Transmitted the Teaching").

Mount Hiei flourished. In its heyday there were 3,000 buildings in the temple complex, and 30,000 monks. Initially the court asserted its superiority to the mountain, but eventually the monasteries took to enforcing demands on the government by mass demonstrations in the streets of the capital, and kept armed retainers to lend force to their claims. Even when Mount Hiei became worldly, though, art, scholarship, and devotion continued to flourish there. The founders of all the new sects of the twelfth and thirteenth century were Tendai monks, which testifies to the vitality of Saichō's lotus even after it had begun to rot.

Whereas Saichō was a good monk and a fine teacher, Kūkai (774–835) was a genius. Born a Nara aristocrat, he studied Buddhism, Confucianism, and Taoism during his teens. He sailed for China in 804, and there studied the Chen-yen (Japanese Shingon) sect, a Vajrayāna system introduced to China about 720. Chen-yen ("True Word") translates *Mantra* ("spell"). The sect's practices include not only mantras, but initiations, ritual gestures, mandalas, and contemplations. Kūkai returned to Japan in 806, and was granted many honors by the emperor. In 816 he founded a monastery on Mount Kōya (see p. 7), which eventually became the headquarters of the Shingon sect. Brilliant disciples flocked to take initiation from Kūkai. He wrote prolifically, and systematized the doctrines that he had received from his teacher in China. He accorded a high place to the arts, and so furthered the aestheticism that distinguishes Japanese Buddhism and general culture. He was famous as a calligrapher. He set up a popular school, and is said to have invented the cursive syllabary (*hiragana*) of forty-seven signs in which, alone or mixed with Chinese characters, Japanese is written. Kūkai died in 835 on Mount Kōya, where he lies buried. There is a folk belief that he is merely sleeping and will rise up again someday. His posthumous title is Kōbō Daishi ("Great Master Who Propagated the Dharma").

Shingon became even more popular than Tendai. Mount Kōya is said to have had 990 temples in its heyday. Shingon teaching was received even on Mount Hiei which rivaled and soon bested Mount Kōya as an esoteric center. By the eleventh century, superstitions and heresies had contaminated Shingon and brought esotericism into disrepute, thus setting the stage for the resolutely exoteric popular sects of the Kamakura period (1192–1338).

By the end of the Heian period, Tendai was coming apart at the seams. Saichō had drawn all the Chinese sectarian teachings into a catholic synthesis, and his successors reached out to encompass even Shintō by identifying its deities with figures in the Buddhist pantheon. But being so all-sided consumed a lot of energy, and slowed the student's progress. So in the twelfth century, earnest monks desiring realization in this life or at least assurance of rebirth in Sukhāvatī took to exclusive pursuit of one or another path. Thus Japan in the twelfth and thirteenth centuries underwent the same sort of fission into sects as China in the sixth and seventh.

The chief social cause for the rise of new sects about 1200 was the shift in balance of power between the capital and the provinces, with a new class of provincial small landowners and samurai claiming their share at court and on the battlefield. They were inclined to support their local temples but were reluctant to give lavishly to the head temples in the distant capital area. Moreover, the new samurai class provided an effective link between the old aristocracy and the peasantry; so that for the first time the higher culture was diffused to the lower classes throughout the country; and some aristocrats, such as the founders of most of the new sects, took the task of popularization seriously.

The cult of Amita (Japanese Amida) was comprised in the Tendai synthesis. Very early, though, a few Tendai monks became exclusive evangelists of the Pure Land teaching. Kūya (903–972) danced in the streets singing simple Japanese hymns about Amida, organized self-help projects among the common people, and even spread the Amidist gospel among the Ainu. Ryōnin (1072–1132) similarly spread the practice of *Nembutsu* (nien-fo) (see pp. 86 ff.) in song, and attracted followers in the court and in the countryside. Genshin (942–1017) was a learned man, and wrote an enormously influential treatise, *The Compendium on Rebirth*. He favored the Nembutsu way not because he considered other paths wrong, but because it was open to all, whether saint or sinner, monk or layman, man or woman, emperor or peasant.

Hōnen (1133–1212), founder of the Jōdo-shū (Pure Land sect), might have followed the same course as Genshin within the Tendai fold if hostile reactionaries had not forced him and his followers into secession. Orphaned in boyhood, he went forth at fifteen and during the next decade, spent on Mount Hiei, he excelled in the wide erudition esteemed by Tendai. Yet he was distressed that he and the people of his age were not able to reach enlightenment or become free from their sins. When he was forty-three, he became convinced through studying Shan-tao (p. 86) and Genshin that only complete reliance on Amida would save him. He wrote a treatise setting forth his faith, but when it was published, monks from Mount Hiei seized and burned all available copies and the printing blocks. He continued to teach his message humbly and without ostentation, and converted an emperor, a regent, noblemen and ladies, monks and commoners. Old-line monks intrigued against him until in 1206, when he was seventy-four, they had him exiled to a remote area from which he was allowed to return only a year before his death.

Shinran (1173–1262), founder of Jōdo-shin-shū (the True Pure Land sect), was one of the disciples exiled at the same time as Hōnen. His early career resembles Hōnen's. His parents died while he was a child. He went to Mount Hiei as a novice and studied there for twenty years, gradually despairing of finding a passable way through the jungle of scholasticism and syncretisms. At twenty-nine, he left Mount Hiei to follow Hōnen. Kwannon (Avalokiteśvara) appeared to him in a dream and told him to marry. With Hōnen's approval, he married a young noblewoman, demonstrating that monasticism was not necessary to salvation, and showing by example that the family should be the center of religious life. Shinran described himself as "neither a monk nor a layman," which aptly categorizes the married clergy of the sect he founded. They continued to live in temples and perform religious services, but they led a family life, and expected the eldest son to take over the temple from his father. But Shin-shū has not proclaimed the household life as an arena in which the great bodhisattva surpasses monks in wisdom and holiness. Shinran considered himself a sinner, and thought of his marriage as an admission of weakness, a recognition that he could not save himself through his own power but must depend on Amida's grace.

Shinran was exiled to the northern province of Echigo, where he propagated the Nembutsu among the common people. Although he was soon pardoned, because Hōnen was dead he did not return to Kyōto, but traveled through the towns and villages of East Japan (Kantō), spread the teaching, and founded temples. During this period he composed his chief work, *Teaching, Practice, Faith and Attainment,* which was published in 1224. In 1235, he returned to Kyōto, and lived quietly there until his death.

Shinran interpreted, elaborated, and in some ways modified Hōnen's teaching. Hōnen had eliminated the element of meditation and merit-gathering from the Nembutsu in order to deepen one's devotion. He held that a single sincere invocation suffices for salvation. Subsequent repetitions are just expressions of gratitude to Amida for assured salvation. The power to exercise faith, says Shinran, is a gift from Amida and not an intrinsic possession of man.

The last point is the general Mahāyāna idea that religious initiative is possible only because the germ of Buddhahood is innate to living beings and is irradiated by the grace of the Buddhas. The radical feature of Shinran's teachings is his utter rejection of the cult of merit, and his apprehension lest the deliberate pursuit of virtue or wisdom either prevent faith or impair one's gratitude to Amida.

Shinran was not a saint in the usual Buddhist sense. He did not keep an austere regimen, he was not celibate, he did not practice meditation, he did not exercise superknowledges, and he used his great erudition only to reinforce the simple Nembutsu faith that he propagated. Nevertheless he is revered by his followers with as much fervor and more sentiment than Vajrayāna accords its great gurus or Zen its famous masters. He was a good and humble man, compassionate and sentimental, sincere in his words and candid about his feelings. Though an aristocrat by birth, he made common cause with the lower classes, shared their way of life, and forewent the display of upper-class learning.

At Shinran's death, there was no Jōdo-shin sect because he had never tried to organize one. He left behind many loose associations of followers, whom his blood descendants organized into a sect. Rennyo (1415–1499) defined the religious position of the school more clearly and shaped its followers into a feudal domain with armies and territorial control. They fortified their temples, and in the sixteenth century withstood Nobunaga's siege of their temple in Osaka for ten years before surrendering only to be slaughtered by the perfidious Shōgun.

Nichiren (1222–1282) was the son of a fisherman. While still a boy he entered a local monastery, and at twenty was studying on Mount Hiei. Like Hōnen and Shinran, he was appalled at the corruption around him, and frustrated with a teaching that offered all paths to all men yet rendered none of them effective. His solution, though, was to return to the root of Chih-i's and

Saichō's teaching, to the *Lotus Sūtra*. He left Mount Hiei after ten years, and went back to his native district. In 1253 he launched his campaign to conquer Japan with the pure *Lotus* gospel. He began chanting "Namu myō-hō-ren-ge-kyō" ("Salutation to the *Lotus Sūtra*"), which formula he held to be a sufficient means of salvation. Anyone who pronounced it would attain Buddhahood, acquire moral virtue, and become on this earth an embodiment of paradise. Nichiren identified himself as an incarnation of the Bodhisattva Superb Conduct, a leader of the bodhisattva hosts whom Śākyamuni summoned out of the earth, and whom he commanded to worship the *Lotus Sūtra*. He was convinced that it was his mission to save the Japanese nation from social and political disorders which he viewed as the consequences of wrong religion. He condemned Shingon because it worshipped Vairocana and neglected Śākyamuni. Amidism he castigated for worshipping Amida rather than Śākyamuni. His criticism of Zen was that it revered only the historical Śākyamuni and not the eternal Buddha of the *Lotus Sūtra*. When he went to Kamakura (the seat of the Shōgun's government) and broadcast his virulent denunciations of all other sects, the government was shocked and the religious world was outraged. He was twice exiled and onced narrowly escaped execution. Each suffering was in his eyes a glorious martyrdom: "Indeed every place where Nichiren encounters perils is a Buddha-land." He achieved recognition as a prophet when the Mongol invasion that he had predicted in 1260 and 1268 was attempted in 1274. Many followers were attracted by his courage, his single-minded zeal, and his vision of Japan as an earthly Buddha-land from which the revived and purified Dharma was to spread throughout the world.

Ch'an was introduced to Japan as early as the seventh century, and taught by a few masters in the eighth and ninth; but it did not catch on until the early Kamakura period, when concentration on a single path came into fashion. Eisai (1141–1215), a Tendai monk and a scholar of Mount Hiei, went to China and trained in the Lin-chi (Rinzai) house, which he established in Japan upon his return in 1191. He won the favor of the Shōguns and forged the alliance with the military class which has ever since been the social foundation of Japanese Zen. By compromising expediently with Tendai and Shingon, he managed to win acceptance for Zen without exacerbating sectarian strife. He appealed to nationalist interests to get Zen accepted, writing a tract, *Propagate Zen, Protect the Country*. He is also venerated as the father of Japanese tea culture. Chinese Ch'an monks engaged in tea planting and also drank tea, as a stimulant to aid meditation and as a social alternative to wine. Kūkai is said to have brought tea from China, but it was Eisai who brought the seeds, planted them in the temple grounds, and fostered the use of the beverage. Fifteenth-century Zen people developed the tea ceremony as a social art and a spiritual discipline. Like flower arrangement, archery, jūdō, and kendō, it is a secularization of Buddhist ritual and contemplation. The goal in these arts it to realize a perfect fusion of aesthetic perception and noumenal awareness, of stillness and motion, of utility and grace, of conformity and spontaneity.

Dōgen (1200–1253), who established the Ts'ao-tung (Sōtō) house of Ch'an in Japan, is revered to this day by Buddhists of all sects and by many non-Buddhists as a great thinker, an admirable man, and a gifted contemplative. His early life is much like that of the other sect-founders of his time. He was born in a noble family, lost his father when he was two and his mother when he was seven, and was awakened religiously by this encounter with suffering and impermanence, reinforced by his mother's deathbed plea that he become a monk. At twelve he left home, and a year later he became a novice on Mount Hiei, where he studied hard until he became engrossed in an enigma: if all living beings have Buddha-nature, then why do the Buddhas and Bodhisattvas all aspire to bodhi and engage in practices? He went around seeking an answer, and so came in 1214 to enter a Zen temple in Kyōto under Eisai's succesor. He and his teacher set out for China in 1223, where he trained under two eminent masters. Dōgen returned to Japan in 1227, and soon settled in a small rural temple where he would be free from the intrigues and contention of temples in Kyōto. He taught zazen, wrote, and attracted so many followers that he had to move several times to more spacious temples. Rather than do battle with the hostile and envious monks of Mount Hiei, he moved to East Japan, was for a while the Shōgun's guest in Kamakura, and settled in the nearby mountain temple, Eihei-ji, which was built especially for him. He was ill for several years with a lung disease, and died at the comparatively young age of fifty-three.

During the Ashikaga period (1333–1568), when the country was divided among powerful feudal lords and, after 1400, rent by civil wars, the two Zen sects were the only major religious bodies that did not resort to arms to defend themselves and to further their cause. Zen monasteries were peaceful havens for thinkers, teachers, and artists. But they were also business entrepreneurs. They engaged in trade with China, maintained their own ships, and sold their imports. Zen monks devised new methods of accounting. Other Zen monks managed academies which taught not only Buddhism but Neo-Confucianism and classical Chinese literature. At the same time, Zen masters wrote tracts in colloquial Japanese, using the forty-seven sign syllabary so that they could be easily read and easily understood when read aloud. Provincial temples disseminated these tracts and their teachings to the people at large.

The Shōgun Nobunaga put an end to Buddhist militancy by destroying all fortified monasteries. He razed the temples on Mount Hiei in 1571, burning the libraries and chapels and beheading or taking captive all the inhabitants. The Tokugawa Shōgunate (1603–1868) gave Japan peace, but at the price of civil and religious liberty. Christianity, which had made headway in the late sixteenth century, was stamped out brutally. As part of the anti-Christian proceedings, every family was required to register as adherents of a Buddhist temple. This "altar-family" system divided the territory and the population into parishes, and incorporated the Buddhist clergy into the state apparatus as census takers, registrars of vital statistics, and government informers. Sects were forbidden to proselytize; conversion from one sect to another was obstructed by bureaucratic means. The government did not contribute financially to the temples, however, but laid the burden on the parishioners. The Buddhist sects became "established" churches, prevented from growth and collapse, spiritually discredited in the eyes of the populace.

Nonetheless, there was a great deal of scholarship, and the sects kept their traditions alive. The temples ran primary schools for children, and deserve much of the credit for the comparatively high rate of literacy with which Japan ended the Tokugawa era. A new Zen sect, the Ōbaku, was introduced from China in the seventeenth century. This stimulated a reform movement within Sōtō Zen in the late seventeenth and early eighteenth centuries. Japan's greatest poet, Matsuo Bashō (1644–1694) was a lay disciple of Zen. In his lapidary haiku, he secularized several salient Buddhist insights and stamped them indelibly into Japanese culture—transiency, loneliness and silence, compassion for living things, awareness of the transcendental in the mundane and natural. Hakuin (1685–1768) revitalized Rinzai Zen, teaching peasants and children and founding a line of eminent meditation masters.

The Meiji Restoration of 1868 was inspired by a Shintō nationalism hostile to Buddhism. After a brief spell of persecution and the expropriation of temple lands, the Buddhists were roused to assert themselves, recovered much of their prestige, and took steps to modernize such as founding schools and universities, and giving the clergy modern educations. The Meiji government decree that the clergy of all sects be allowed to marry has been observed so well that nowadays there are very few monks in Japan except for young men in training. The various sects have taken on a panoply of modern lay organizations, Sunday schools, boy scout troops, meditation clubs, and young people's societies. There are many popular Buddhist magazines, popular books on Buddhism and translations of the Sūtras are found in every neighborhood bookstore, and a plethora of scholarly books and journals continues to be published. Busloads of tourists visit the old temples of Nara. Kōya-san and Hiei-zan are accessible by cablecar, and women are no longer excluded from their premises. The old sects possess an impressive number of temples, clerics, and lay followers. They are apprehensive about the new lay movements such as Sōka-gakkai and Risshō-kōseikai, which bypass the old ecclesiastical apparatus and often use aggressive methods that are offensive to traditional Buddhists. These new sects have attracted millions of members and have placed Buddhism in the central arena of national life for the first time since the sixteenth century. But they are not likely to jeopardize the future existence of the historic sects. Since the Nara period, no sect that acquired independent institutional status has ever become extinct.

Southeast Asia

For over two millenia the history of Ceylon has been a continual struggle against foreign invaders—Tamils, Portuguese, Dutch, British. Theravāda has been closely linked with the fortunes of the Sinhala monarchy, and its conservative, archaistic character has been preserved through the common efforts of kings and elders to guard a perennially threatened national heritage. Time and again, even the ordination lineage was in danger of extinction, and valid succession had to be obtained from Burma (1065, 1475, and 1801 A.D.) and Thailand (1753 A.D.). The two high points were the reigns of King Mahānāma (409–431), when the illustrious Indian bhikṣu Buddhaghosa resided and wrote in Ceylon, and of King Vijayabāhu, who undertook in 1065 to revive the religion, restored the valid ordination succession, and appointed the first Sangharāja to oversee the entire Saṅgha. The Portuguese (1505–1658) seized the lowlands, destroyed monasteries, and forcibly converted people to Catholicism. The Sinhala kings withdrew to Kandy, where they ruled from 1592 till 1815, supporting Buddhism insofar as their circumstances and resources would permit. Under the treaty by which they took over from the monarchy, the British were bound to protect Buddhism, but evangelical Christian missionaries pressured the government into relinquishing all Buddhist affairs, and then proceeded to attack Buddhism. Before long, Buddhist spokesmen replied, lay associations were formed, training centers for monks were established, and a revival was under way. Two Westerners who aided the cause of Buddhism are especially revered in Ceylon: Henry Olcott, an American Theosophist who traveled around the country exhorting the people to revive their historic religion, and T. W. Rhys Davids, founder of the Pali Text Society, who by rendering Gautama's teachings admirable in European eyes gave confidence and pride to the peoples who had preserved them.

The early history of Buddhism in Burma is unknown. Burmese chronicles say that Buddhaghosa visited the country and introduced Pali scholarship. By the fifth and sixth centuries, both Mahāyāna and Hīnayāna had found their way in, coming apparently from the Pallava kingdom in South India. From the ninth century onward, Mahāyāna and Vajrayāna came in from the Pāla kingdom in Bengal and Bihar. The chronicles say that King Anawrahta, ruling in Pagān, wanted to introduce Theravāda, and conquered the kingdom of Thaton in South Burma when its ruler refused the copies of the *Tripiṭika* that Anawrahta requested. It is said that he drove out the Vajrayāna monks, yet archaeological evidence shows that Mahāyāna flourished as never before alongside Theravāda under the Anawrahta dynasty (1044–1283). The Mongols sacked Pagan in 1287, and the city with its nine thousand pagodas and temples was abandoned. In the following centuries, the country was divided between rival kings, Mahāyāna dwindled away, and Theravāda survived. A new dynasty ruled a reunited Burma from 1752 to 1886, when Britain deposed the king and annexed Burma to India. Under the monarchy, the Saṅgha was favored and grew, in spite of a petty controversy over whether the monk should wear his upper robe over both shoulders or only over the left. The issue bitterly divided the Saṅgha until the king decreed in 1784 that the both-shoulders faction was right. Pali studies flourished in the nineteenth century, and the

Suttas were translated into Burmese. The king appointed a hierarchy headed by his chaplain to regulate the affairs of the order. After the British took over, they declined to appoint a new Saṅgharāja when the old one died, but eventually arranged for the whole Saṅgha to elect a superior for itself. When outside authority was thus removed, discipline in the monasteries deteriorated. Monks played a prominent part in the early days of the independence movement, later faded into the background, and emerged after independence as an ecclesiastical lobby.

Buddhism is an integral part of Burmese village life, where the village vihāra coexists with shrines to the *nats* ("spirits") whom the people petition for mundane favors just as early Indian Buddhists propitiated the devas. Dharma-study and meditation centers flourish in the cities, and the place of Buddhism in the nation is secure and paramount.

The history of Buddhism in Cambodia, Thailand, and Laos is similar to that of Burma. Mahāyāna and Hinduism flourished side by side in the Khmer empire from the fifth till the fifteenth centuries, when Theravāda, introduced under Thai influence, supplanted both its rivals. The Thais had been exposed to Mahāyāna before the thirteenth century A.D., when they moved south from China into Siam, where the Burmese had already established Theravāda in the eleventh century. Under royal patronage, Theravāda gradually acquired the temples and the devotees from Hinduism and Mahāyāna, and nowadays the Hindu substratum in Thai popular religion is quite attenuated.

Indonesia was Indianized by merchants, Brāhmans, and adventurers in the first centuries of the Christian era. By the fifth century A.D., Buddhism and Hinduism were established in Java and Sumatra. The eighth-century Borobudur Stūpa in Java is the greatest and most glorious of all stūpas. Its circumambulation path leads past two thousand and more reliefs depicting scenes from Śākyamuni's life, the Jātakas, and the Mahāyāna Sūtras. The ascent is a ritual journey through the triple world, out of saṃsāra and into nirvāṇa. Vajrayāna came in from Bengal after the seventh century, and flourished until it was suppressed by Islam in the fourteenth and fifteenth centuries.

Tibet

Tibet entered history in the seventh century A.D. when a line of kings became firmly established, enlarged their domain, and came to the notice of Chinese historians. About 632, according to tradition, King Song-tsen-gam-po (Srong-btsan-sgam-po)[1] sent an emissary to Kashmir to learn writing and devise a script for Tibetan. Buddhism seems to have entered Tibet from Kashmir and Khotan during this king's reign. For some time the new religion made little progress. In the mid-seventh century, there were faction fights between pro-

[1] Tibetan words are given first in a roughly phonetic spelling, and then in a mechanical transliteration of the Tibetan orthography, which represents the pronunciation of a thousand years ago.

and anti-Buddhist nobles at the court. When the Buddhists won, the king and his ministers brought in the Indian master Śāntarakṣita, who stayed a while, went to Nepal, and came back later for a more successful second visit. At the same time a famous but historically vague figure, Padmasambhava, arrived from Uḍḍiyāna (Swat), a noted Tantric center. He ranks as one of the eighty-four Siddhas (Tantric saints), and is credited in Tibetan tradition with fabulous wonder-working. The sect of the Nying-ma-pas (Rnying-ma-pa, "Ancient One") claim him as their founder, though he stayed in Tibet just long enough to cofound with Śāntarakṣita the Tibetan Saṅgha and the first monastery (787). A Chinese Ch'an master named Mahāyāna came to the court and made many converts. A debate was held before the king in 794 or thereabouts, in which Śāntarakṣita's school vigorously attacked the Ch'an faction and succeeded in getting the king to banish the Chinese. Despite continual intercourse with the Chinese, Tibetan Buddhism has ever since been based on that of India.

The development of Tibetan Buddhism has been an interaction between scholar-monks leading a conventional celibate life (typified by Śāntarakṣita) and wonder-working yogins wandering freely, often not wearing the monastic robe and not bound to celibacy (typified by Padma-sambhava). "Lama" is just the Tibetan translation for "guru," and either an eminent monk or an outstanding householder yogin may bear the title.

The work of translating scriptures went forward rapidly in the early ninth century under the patronage of the pious King Ral-pa-can. A commission of Indian and Tibetan scholars standardized the technical terminology and published a Sanskrit-Tibetan glossary. It was decided that with few exceptions texts would only be translated from Sanskrit, and works previously translated from vernacular versions were retranslated fom Sanskrit. The Tibetan language was stretched, bent, and molded to express a wide range of alien contents and styles. Tibetan translations are often opaque, but they are marvelously consistent and usually match the original point for point.

The king's chief minister, a monk named "Virtue," was first slandered and then executed. Pro-Buddhist nobles murdered the king, whose vicious brother Lang-dar-ma (Glang-dar-ma, 836–842) succeeded him and by persecution eliminated organized Buddhism from Central Tibet. Lang-dar-ma himself was murdered by a monk, but the damage was not repaired for generations. The line of kings terminated, and the religion survived as mundane magic practiced by itinerant yogis. Refugee monks spread Buddhism in other parts of the country, notably in East Tibet (Kham). A descendent of Lang-dar-ma established a strong kingdom in West Tibet in the tenth century, and his successors undertook to promote the Dharma. They chose twenty-one Tibetan boys and sent them to India to learn Sanskrit, study doctrine, and persuade Indian masters to come to Tibet. All but two of the boys died from heat and disease on the Indian plains. Of the two boys who survived to become scholars, the more famous was Rin-chen Sangpo (Bzang-po, 958–1055). The illustrious Bengali scholar Atīśa (982–1054), after much persuasion, came to West

Tibet in 1042. He was well versed in exoteric and esoteric teachings, and his career crowned the renaissance of doctrine studies in Tibet. He is also famed for the most gracious of all recorded first reactions to Tibetan buttered tea: "This cup contains the elixir of the wish-granting tree."

By this time, Central Tibet had recovered from the persecution. Monks had come in from Kham and rebuilt the monasteries, and a new line of kings (also descended from Lang-dar-ma) were furnishing patronage. Atīśa's chief disciple Drom ('Brom) persuaded him to go to Lhasa, where he spent the rest of his life conferring Tantric initiations and translating. Drom, though a layman, was Atīśa's spiritual heir, and founded the Ka-dam-pa (Bka'-gdams-pa) lineage, the first Tibetan sect whose historic beginnings (unlike Nying-ma-pa) are clear.

Drok-mi ('Brog-mi), a contemporary of Atīśa's, studied in the Tantric university of Vikramaśīla for eight years, then returned to Tibet, where in 1073 he founded the monastery of Sa-skya, whose abbots possessed great learning and temporal power during the twelfth and thirteenth centuries. Sa-kya-pa (Sa-skya-pa) abbots are permitted to marry, and the succession passes either from father to son or from uncle to nephew. The abbot 'Phags-pa (1235–1280), continuing the relations his uncle had established with the Mongols, became prelate to Kublai Khan, from whom he received temporal jurisdiction over all of Tibet.

Mar-pa (1012–1097) was a disciple of the great Bengali adept Nāropa, under whom he trained at Nālandā. Returning to Tibet, he took a wife whom he called Nairātmyā, as she also served as his prajñā in the rites of Hevajra (see p. 75). Mar-pa was a man of strong character and strong passions, wrathful and possessive. Only when his own son died did he stop denying the spiritual succession to his long-suffering and gifted disciple Milarepa (Mi-la ras-pa, "the Cotton-clad Mila").

Milarepa (1040–1123) is the most popular saint and the greatest poet of Tibet, as well as the Second Patriarch of the Kargyüpa (Bka'-rgyud-pa) sect founded by Mar-pa. As a youth, he learned magic in order to take revenge on a wicked uncle who had dispossessed and maltreated Mila's widowed mother. Having destroyed his enemies, he was seized by remorse and sought first to expiate his bad karma and then to attain liberation. At thirty-eight he became Mar-pa's disciple. For six years the master put him through cruel ordeals before finally granting him the initiation he sought. Milarepa spent the rest of his life meditating in the caves and wandering on the slopes of the High Himalayas (Kailāśa, Everest). He gradually attracted a following, converted many disciples, and worked wonders for people's benefit. His numerous songs express not only profound Dharma, but the unearthly atmosphere of his mountain home, and the cruel rigors and high ecstasies of the ascetic life.

The Kargyüpa line was continued by Gam-po-pa (Sgam-po-pa, 1079–1153), who at thirty-two heard of Milarepa from a beggar and acquired his teachings in thirteen months' study. After Gam-po-pa, the sect split into four branches, one of which converted Bhutan in the seventeenth century, and another of which was favored by the Mongol and Ming emperors of China.

The Tibetan scriptures were collected and edited to form a Canon by Butön (Bu-ston, 1290–1364). This Canon consists of two collections: the *Kanjur* (Bka'-'gyur) which comprises the Vinaya, Sūtras, and Tantras, and the *Tenjur* (Bstan-'gyur) which contains treatises, commentaries, and works on auxiliary sciences such as grammar, astrology, and medicine. The first printed Kanjur was completed in Peking in 1411, and the first complete printings of the Canon in Tibet were at Narthang (Snar-thang)—the Kanjur (100 volumes) in 1731 and the Tenjur (225 volumes) in 1742.

The scene in the early fourteenth century was a welter of sects and subsects. Besides the Ka-dam-pas, the Sa-kya-pas and the various Kar-gyü-pa branches, there were the Shi-je-pas (Zhi-byed-pa, "Tranquilizer" or "Peacemaker"), a sect of yogins founded in the late eleventh century by the Indian master Pha-dam-pa Sanggye (Pha-dam-pa Sangs-rgyas, "Holy Father Buddha"), and the Nying-ma-pas, revitalized by Guru Chö-wang (Chos-dbang, 1212–1273) who discovered (or claimed to discover) "hidden scriptures" deposited by Padma-sambhava and others. Except for the Ka-dam-pas, these sects were lax in discipline, and all were given to politics and magic.

Tsong-kha-pa (1357–1419) was a native of Northeast Tibet, where he became a novice in boyhood and received Tantric initiations. (Strong meat for little boys!) He was then sent by his teacher to Central Tibet where he studied the exoteric Mahāyāna treatises for years and visited all the notable centers of learning. He was particularly fond of Logic and Vinaya. He took full ordination at age twenty-five, began to teach, and through the good offices of a guru was able to "meet" Mañjuśrī. In 1393 he had just eight pupils. By 1409, he had a multitude of disciples and controlled the main temple of Lhasa. His new sect, the Gelukpa (Dge-lugs-pa, "Partisan of Virtue"), professed to continue the strict discipline of the Ka-dam-pas, laid equal stress on the exoteric and the esoteric teachings, and implemented a regular curriculum of systematic doctrinal studies leading to the degree of *Geshe* (Dge-shes, "spiritual friend"), equivalent to a doctorate in philosophy or divinity. Three large Gelukpa monasteries were founded near Lhasa in 1409, 1416, and 1419. Tsongkhapa was a brilliant scholar, an excellent organizer, and a reformer. His monks had to forego liquor, sex, evening meals, and long naps. He condemned worldly magic, and his sect practices the Tantras only as a means to enlightenment.

Tsongkhapa's third successor was his nephew Gendün truppa (Dge-'dun grub-pa), who took office in 1438. He was accepted as an incarnation of Avalokiteśvara, and so started the line of Dalai Lamas. As the intermediate state is believed to last forty-nine days, a search party looks for a child born that long after the death of a Dalai Lama, guided by whatever indications the dying Incarnation has left concerning his next appearance, and by the pronouncements of the state oracle. The searchers look for certain physical signs on the infant, prodigies at the time of his birth (for example, a tree that blossoms in winter), and ability to recognize objects belonging to the previous Incarnation. Once the right child is found, he is brought to Lhasa and carefully educated for his future role. Meanwhile, regents rule on his behalf.

The third Dalai Lama (1543–1588) converted the Mongols for the second and last time. He is said to have met the pagan gods of the Mongols, converted them, and made them into Dharma-protectors. The fourth Dalai Lama (1589–1616) turned out providentially to be the grandson of the grand chief of the Mongols. The fifth Dalai Lama (1617–1682) was a great scholar, surprisingly well versed in Nyingmapa literature. He was an energetic and shrewd politician, and with the aid of Mongol armies overthrew the enemies of his sect and became the temporal as well as the spiritual ruler of Tibet. His repressive measures forced many clerics of other sects to take refuge in outlying areas of Tibet, in Sikkim and Bhutan. The new Manchu dynasty in China confirmed the Dalai Lama's power and used him and his successors to keep Tibet quiet and safe for China, just as the Dalai Lamas used their status and their wiles to keep the Chinese out of Tibet as much as possible. The sixth Dalai Lama (1683–1706) was a drinker and girl-chaser and the reputed author of a collection of love songs. He came from a family of Nyingmapas, and his apparent debauchery seems to have been part of an attempt to revive the old Tantric ways. Intense opposition sprang up. A conclave of lamas decided that Avalokiteśvara had abandoned the body of the incumbent and had entered another lama. Finally a Mongol army burst into Lhasa, killed the regent, and captured the Dalai Lama alive. He died in captivity, perhaps murdered. Subsequent Dalai Lamas were loyal Gelukpas, and kept out of trouble with the Chinese. The ninth through the twelfth Incarnations died in boyhood. The thirteenth Dalai Lama (1874–1933) survived the perils of childhood only to get caught in international politics. He had to flee to Mongolia when the British sent an army to Lhasa in 1904, and in 1910 he fled to India to escape the Chinese, returning in 1912 after the Manchu dynasty fell. The fourteenth Dalai Lama (1935–) was enthroned in 1950, one year before the Chinese Communists marched in and occupied his country. He fled to India during the anti-Chinese uprisings of 1959. While he lives in exile and serves as *de facto* leader for the tens of thousands of Tibetan refugees, the Chinese grind away the remnants of a medieval culture and religion that, sordid politics notwithstanding, produced a brave, cheerful, and courteous people, many great scholars, and in each generation a few real saints.

5.
Past, Present and Future

Buddhism, like the other higher religions, has been slow to perceive that modern civilization is radically different from that of any preceding age, that it is not just machines and techniques, and that it is no use hoping that this menace will go away and leave traditional religions alone if only they ignore it or make a truce with it or try to subordinate it by declaring their jurisdiction over spiritual matters and relegating science to the lower, worldly sphere. Yet the Buddhist responses to the waves of social and cultural change originating in Europe have been distinctive in some ways, and have conformed to patterns well instanced in the Buddhist past.

From the first, the Saṅgha has seen itself as parallel to the state, subject to the Dharma-king and claiming the adherence of people who also owe allegiance to the king of the land. Conflict of duties has usually been avoided by specifying which authority is to prevail in which sphere. Nonetheless, certain tensions in moral matters have been perennially unresolved. Strict observance of the precepts is incompatible with statecraft and with the life-styles of ruling classes. A few devout rulers have renounced war, for example, but no Buddhist state has ever given up the use of armies and police. Moreover, the rulers have often had to use force to quell violence and corruption in the monasteries themselves. Eventually all Buddhist states established the post of Saṅgha-director so as to incorporate the church into the bureaucracy and prevent it from becoming a rival political power. Yet the chief source of disorder in the Order has been the patronage of princes, who by giving more lavishly than wisely have made the monastic life a haven for drones and a temptation to the ambitious. After the tax and rent collectors were through with them, peasants did not have enough surplus left to support a learned Saṅgha. Where commerce flourished, merchant guilds usually financed Buddhist activities; but merchants often practiced emulative donation, thus making the Saṅgha too wealthy for its own good. Besides, interregional commerce was allied with the kings, and did not constitute an independent counterbalance. When a strong state such as imperial China decided to exclude the Buddhist community from a major role in national life, there was no social bloc strong enough to stop it. Under the circumstances, it is not only the reluctance of bhikṣus to dictate morals to the laity which has restrained the Dharma-masters, with a few notable exceptions, from denouncing the tyranny and licentiousness of rulers.

Colonial rule, secular governments, and land reform have stripped the

Order of state patronage and economic self-sufficiency in almost every Buddhist country. The shock of losing their lands and privileges dissipated lethargy, and the need to find a new donorship base stimulated revivals that the Christian missionary and Western secular challenges then enhanced. The Saṅgha typically affiliated itself with the national bourgeoisie that rose in the early stages of modernization. Where there was no bourgeoisie, as in Tibet, there was no revival. Where the modernizing elite already had a secular ideology, as in Japan and China, Buddhism had to stand on the sidelines, where many of the old-fashioned gentry, forsaking a discredited Confucianism, rallied to the most "modern" and international element in their national heritage.

Everywhere, Buddhists have been staunch nationalists, have taken part in anticolonial movements, have claimed to be custodians of the national culture, and have longed to reestablish the old symbiosis between Saṅgha and state. In a secular age, this dream is not going to come true, but nationalist sentiment will undoubtedly maintain Buddhism wherever freedom of religion prevails. However, the Dharma is presently too weak, and the Saṅgha, too dependent, to exercise moral authority and restrain political excesses. Most citizens are nationalists first, and Buddhists second, if at all.

The traditional case for public donorship was that Buddhism protects the community from disasters and assures prosperity. The original standpoint was that ethics is a better magic than magic, but in course of time meritorious deeds came to be prized more for their unseen effects than for discernible ethical consequences. The expectation of miraculous "advantages here and now" is still lively among the culturally disadvantaged, but when a modern government sponsors a Buddhist enterprise—publication of the Canon, or an international conference—it is thinking not of earning merit for the nation but of fulfilling cultural responsibilities and gaining popularity.

Modern educated Buddhists tend to jettison the magical component. They say that it is a separable accretion of superstition. This is historically true for many specific practices, but we have seen that the realm of the spirits and the preternatural operations of karma are integral to the earliest known Buddhist world view. Modern Buddhist thinkers (with some exceptions) are ashamed to believe something that is out of fashion in the West, yet have not squarely faced the intellectual and practical consequences of rejecting the belief. Buddhism cannot be reduced to a humanism without radical structural changes. Apologists, tailoring their theses to needs and opportunities, have usually insisted that Buddhism is scientific, and have played down anything that does not fit the claim. This has widened the gulf between intellectuals and lower-class devotees, for whom the magical is the most meaningful part of the religion.

There has not yet been a cogent attempt to update the intellectual foundations of Buddhism. The Theravāda clergy have mostly adhered to a fundamentalist position, thus foregoing fruitful two-way interchange with the secular world of today. But things are changing, and lay scholars plus a few monks in Ceylon, for example, are pursuing historically critical and philosophically rigorous studies. Japanese Buddhist intellectuals adopted an eclectic modernism almost a century ago, and have striven to keep up with international fashions in religion and philosophy while avoiding decisive engagements with basic problems. Thus there has been almost no creative application of their massive historical scholarship. The "new religions" have developed their ideas by methods that were second-rate even in the thirteenth century, but in demonstrating that a radical break with venerable institutions can lead to success, they may be liberating as yet undetected creative energies.

Some decades ago, meditation was commonly neglected by Buddhists who were trying to become modern, because until recently Westerners have scorned it, alleging that quietism and subjectivism are morbid and sap the will to act. Political independence movements have lessened this responsiveness to Western disapproval. And now that psychiatry has sparked a cult of self-awareness in the West, meditation is coming back into fashion in every part of Buddhist Asia that Marxism does not hold in thrall to nineteenth-century European attitudes. In Japan, where contemplative arts became secularized in the Middle Ages, lay meditation movements have made considerable headway, and have strengthened the still vigorous core of monastic meditation. The Theravāda meditation revival is an urban appropriation of a tradition that survived precariously among jungle hermits. The motive force is humanistic: to alleviate the tensions of urban and industrial life, and to find secure values by gaining insight.

A hundred years ago, the chief service role of the Saṅgha was performing ceremonies, especially funeral and memorial rites. Nowadays this function has dwindled greatly as ritual simplification keeps pace with declining belief in unseen forces. The second service role of the Order was elementary education, which has now been taken over by public schools. But as the old needs wane, new needs grow. In some places, the Saṅgha has become an educational entrepreneur, running modern-style private schools and universities. Conversely, some public school systems include religious instruction and so give secular jobs to monks.

A need closer to the Saṅgha's proper role is that for relief from anxiety, agitation, and confusion. Though the secular palliatives—art and literature, philosophy, psychiatry, tranquilizers, and psychedelics—are moderately efficacious, some of them are very expensive, and all stop short of the moral, intellectual, and spiritual integration that is the goal of the Buddhist life.

In past ages, revitalization of Buddhism has happened when a widespread demand is met by outstanding holy men. Today there is certainly a worldwide spiritual need. There is also an evergrowing study and dissemination of the Dharma. This is creating a clientele ready to respond if, out of season in this Last Age, a great holy man should appear.

SELECTED READINGS

Chapter 1

de Berval, René, ed., *Présence du Bouddhisme*. Saigon: France-Asie, 1959. Articles of varying quality in French and English on Buddhism in most countries.

Hanh, Thich Nhat, *Vietnam, the Lotus in the Sea of Fire*. London: SCM Press, 1967. Excellent presentation of the Vietnamese Buddhist story by a Vietnamese monk.

Japan, the Official Guide, 9th ed., edited by the Tourist Industry Bureau, Ministry of Transportation. Tokyo: Japan Travel Bureau, 1962. A solid data bank, good on temples and with many maps.

Pratt, James B., *A Pilgrimage of Buddhism and a Buddhist Pilgrimage*. New York: Macmillan, 1928. A canny Yankee scholar's tour of Buddhist Asia.

Schechter, Jerrold, *The New Face of Buddha*. New York: Coward-McCann, 1967. Firsthand reporting by a journalist who has seen much and understood very little.

Valisinha, Devapriya, *Buddhist Shrines in India*. Colombo: Maha Bodhi Society of Ceylon, 1948. A handy pilgrim's guide.

Williams, Rushbrook, ed., *A Handbook for Travellers in India, Pakistan, Burma and Ceylon*. London: John Murray, 1962. Solid and old-fashioned, with much archaeological information.

Chapter 2

General

Basham, A. L., *The Wonder that was India*. New York: Grove Press, 1959. A survey of the culture of the Indian subcontinent before the coming of the Muslims: a many-splendored classic.

Conze, Edward, ed., *Buddhist Texts through the Ages* (hereafter referred to as *Texts*). Oxford: Cassirer, 1954. Also Harper Torchbooks. Includes 100 pages of excerpts from the Pali by I. B. Horner.

Foucher, A., *The Life of the Buddha*. Middletown, Conn., 1963. A poor English translation of *La Vie du Bouddha*, Paris: Payot, 1949. The author, a great historian of Buddhist art, expresses many dubious opinions on doctrine and religion.

Horner, I. B., *The Living Thoughts of Gotama the Buddha*. London: Cassell, 1948. Excellent anthology from the Pali, with a brilliant introduction by Ananda K. Coomaraswamy.

Nārada Thera, *The Buddha and His Teachings*. Colombo, Ceylon: Vajirārāma, 1964. Good translations of basic Pali texts, with authoritative commentary by a Theravāda scholar-monk.

Thapar, Romila, *A History of India*, Vol. I. Baltimore: Penguin, 1966. Readable, up-to-date, sound. Maps on pp. 61, 100, 116–17, 182–83.

Thomas, E. J., *The History of Buddhist Thought* (hereafter referred to as *History*). London: Routledge & Kegan Paul, 1933. Very good as an account of Early Buddhist thought according to the Pali Canon.

———, *The Life of the Buddha as Legend and History* (hereafter referred to as *Life*). London: Routledge & Kegan Paul, 1927. Readable, scholarly, standard.

Warren, Henry C., *Buddhism in Translations,* 1st ed. Cambridge, Mass.: Harvard University Press, Harvard Oriental Series, 1896. Also in paperback. Judicious selections from Pali texts in graceful but dated translations.

The Upaniṣads

Basham, *op. cit.,* pp. 232–243, 247–256.

Keith, Arthur Berriedale, *The Religion and Philosophy of the Vedas and Upanishads* (hereafter referred to as *Religion*). Harvard Oriental Series, 2 vols., 1925. Authoritative, difficult.

Radhakrishnan, Sarvepalli, *The Principal Upaniṣads.* London: Allen & Unwin, 1953. Introduction, texts and good translations.

Radhakrishnan, Sarvepalli and Charles A. Moore, eds., *A Source Book in Indian Philosophy.* Princeton, N.J.: Princeton University Press, 1957. A standard textbook and reference work. Selections from Upaniṣads, pp. 37–96.

On early Indian religion, also consult Thomas J. Hopkins, *The Hindu Tradition,* in this same Dickenson series, "The Religious Life of Man."

The Ascetic Movement

Basham, *op. cit.,* pp. 243–247, 287–297.

Davids, C. A. F. Rhys, "Asceticism (Buddhist)," in Hastings' *Encyclopaedia of Religion and Ethics* (*ERE*), vol. 2, pp. 69*b*–71*b*.

Eliade, Mircea, *Yoga: Immortality and Freedom.* New York: Pantheon, 1958. Asceticism, pp. 101–111 and *passim.*

Jacobi, Hermann, "Jainism," in *ERE,* vol. 7, pp. 465*a*–474*a*.

Jayatilleke, K. N., *Early Buddhist Theory of Knowledge.* London: Allen & Unwin, 1963. A masterpiece. Sometimes hard reading, always rewarding. Excellent survey of śramaṇa thought, pp. 69–168.

Gautama the Buddha: Birth to First Sermon

Johnston, E. H., *The Buddhacarita, or Acts of the Buddha.* Part II, Translation. Calcutta: Baptist Mission Press, 1936. Chapters 1–14 in scholarly and readable translation. The rest of the *Buddhacarita* is translated by Johnston in *Acta Orientalia,* XV (1937).

Nārada, *op. cit.,* pp. 1–64, 318–331.

Warren, *op. cit.,* pp. 38–83, 331–349.

Interpretation of the Enlightenment

Eliade, *op. cit.,* pp. 318–340.

The Twelve Preconditions

Jayatilleke, *op. cit.,* pp. 445–457. Sets Keith straight.

Keith, Arthur Berriedale, *Buddhist Philosophy in India and Ceylon.* 1st ed., 1923. Reprint Chowkhamba, Banaras, 1963. Masterly but quirky. Causation, pp. 96–114.

Nārada, *op. cit.,* pp. 418–431.

Thomas, *Thought,* pp. 58–70.

Warren, *op. cit.,* pp. 165–208.

The Hierarchy of Beings
Keith, *Religion:* Indra, pp. 124–133; Gandharvas and Apsarases, pp. 179–184; demons, pp. 231–242; spirits of the dead, pp. 403–432; on Brahmā, see "Brahman (m.)" in the index.
Nārada, *op. cit.,* pp. 432–452.
Renou, Louis et Jean Filliozat, *L'Inde Classique.* Tome I (Nos. 1–1357). Paris: Payot, 1947. Tome II (Nos. 1358–2494). Paris: Imprimerie Nationale, 1953. The standard topical encyclopedia of Indology. Tome II, pp. 315–608, presents everything the fledgling scholar should learn about Buddhism, and much that is new to veterans. On pantheon, see Nos. 1029, 1077–9, 1086–7, 2266–72.
Warren, *op. cit.,* pp. 289–291, 308–330.

Commentary on the First Sermon
Dutt, Nalinaksha, *Aspects of Mahāyāna Buddhism and its Relations to Hīnayāna* (hereafter referred to as *Aspects*). London: Luzac, 1930. A great book. Doctrine of *nirvāṇa,* pp. 129–202.
Jayatilleke, *op. cit.,* pp. 382–401. On faith.
Nārada, *op. cit.,* pp. 74–102.
Poussin, Louis de La Vallée, *Nirvāṇa.* Paris, 1925. His mature view, well developed and qualified.
———, *The Way to Nirvāṇa.* Cambridge, 1917. Popular lectures by one of the greatest modern Buddhologists.
Robinson, Richard H., "The Classical Indian Axiomatic," in *Philosophy East and West,* XVII (1967), pp. 139–154. On being, non-being, and the Middle Way.
Stcherbatsky, Theodore, *The Conception of Buddhist Nirvāṇa.* Leningrad: Office of the Academy of Sciences of the U.S.S.R., 1927. An attack on La Vallée Poussin by another great master.
Warren, *op. cit.,* pp. 380–391, 117–128.
Welbon, Guy Richard, *The Buddhist Nirvāṇa and its Western Interpreters.* University of Chicago Press, 1968. A readable and discerning history of the West's intellectual encounter with Buddhism as instanced in the problem of *nirvāṇa.*

Founding the Saṅgha
Nārada, *op. cit.,* pp. 103–225.
Thomas, *Life,* pp. 89–142.

The Parinirvāṇa
Nārada, pp. 233–269.
Thomas, *Life,* pp. 143–164.
Warren, *op. cit.,* pp. 95–110.

Chapter 3

Formation of the Canon
Conze, Edward, *Thirty Years of Buddhist Studies.* Oxford: Cassirer, 1967. A collection of articles. The first, "Recent Progress in Buddhist Studies," first published 1959–60, resumes the state of scholarship on the Buddhist scriptures.
Inde Classique, Nos. 1940–2169. The best scholarly précis on Buddhist literature.

Macdonell, A. A., "Literature (Buddhist)," *ERE,* vol. 8, pp. 85*a*–89*b*.
Nārada, *op. cit.*, pp. 270–278.
Thomas, *Thought,* pp. 261–287. A survey of the Pali Canon and other Buddhist scriptures.

Early Schisms and Sects

Aung, Shwe Zan, trans. and C. A. F. Rhys Davids, ed., *Compendium of Philosophy.* London: Luzac, 1910 and 1956. Translation of the *Abhidhammattha-saṅgaha,* a medieval Theravāda textbook on Abhidhamma. Excellent introduction and notes.
Bareau, André, *Les Sectes bouddhiques du Petit Véhicule.* Saigon: École Française d'Extrême-Orient, 1955. A definitive scholarly work.
Conze, Edward, *Buddhist Thought in India* (hereafter referred to as *Thought*). London: Allen & Unwin, 1962. Also Harper Torchbooks. The best on the subject in English. Hīnayāna sects, pp. 119–191.
Funahashi, Issai, *et al.,* "Abhidharmakośa-śāstra," in *Encyclopaedia of Buddhism* (*EB*), vol. 1, pp. 58*a*–63*a*.
Karunaratne, W. S., H. G. A. van Zeyst, and Kōgen Mizuno, "Abhidhamma," fasc. 1, pp. 37*b*–49*a,* in *EB,* ed. G. P. Malalasekera, published by the Government of Ceylon. Fascicule 1 appeared in 1961. Subsequent fascicules come out from time to time. This encyclopedia is an outstanding piece of Asian international cooperation. The best articles in it are really excellent.
Kao Kuan-ju, "Abhidharma-mahāvibhāṣā," *EB,* vol. 1, pp. 80*a*–84*a*.
Mizuno Kōgen, "Abhidharma Literature," *EB,* vol. 1, pp. 64*b*–80*a*.
Poussin, Louis de La Vallée, *L'Abhidharmakośa de Vasubandhu.* Paris: Geuthner, 1923–1931. Annotated translation of the crowning masterpiece of the Abhidharma movement.
Stcherbatsky, Theodore, *The Central Conception of Buddhism.* London: Royal Asiatic Society, 1923. Reprint Susil Gupta, Calcutta, 1956. A brief interpretive exposition of the *Abhidharmakośa*'s doctrine.

Aśoka

Basham, *op. cit.*, pp. 48–57.

Religious Life in the Early Centuries

Anesaki, M., "Ethics and Morality (Buddhist)," *ERE,* vol. 5, pp. 477*b*–455*b*.
Conze, Edward, *Buddhist Scriptures.* Penguin, 1959. Morality, pp. 69–97.
Geden, A. S., "Monasticism (Buddhist)," *ERE,* vol. 8, pp. 797*a*–802*b*.
Horner, *Living Thoughts,* pp. 74–75, 88–138.
Vinaya, Pātimokkha, *Sacred Books of the East* (*SBE*), vol. 13, pp. 1–69.
Warren, *op. cit.*, pp. 91–94, 392–421, 441–481.

The Rise of Mahāyāna

Bareau, *op. cit.*, pp. 296–305.
Conze, *Thought,* pp. 195–204.
Dutt, *Aspects.*
Lamotte, Étienne, "Sur la formation du Mahāyāna," *Asiatica* (*Festschrift F. Weller*). Leipzig, 1954. Pp. 381–386.

The Teaching of Emptiness

Conze, Edward, *Buddhist Wisdom Books*. London: Allen & Unwin, 1958. Contains Diamond-Cutter Sūtra and Heart Sūtra, translation with commentary.

———, *Selected Sayings from the Perfection of Wisdom*. London: The Buddhist Society, 1955.

———, *Thought*, pp. 238–249.

Lamotte, Étienne, *L'Enseignement de Vimalakīrti* (Vimalakīrtinirdeśa). Louvain: Publications Universitaires, 1962. Excellent translation, with copious notes and introduction, of one of the most important and well-written Mahāyāna Sūtras.

Murti, T. R. V., *The Central Philosophy of Buddhism*. London: Allen & Unwin, 1955. A great book on Mādhyamika, somewhat obscured by the author's thinking in Sanskrit and writing in the vocabulary of 1910-ish British idealism.

Robinson, Richard H., *Classical Indian Philosophy*. Madison, Wis.: College Printing and Typing, 1968. Summary of Mādhyamika on pp. 71–79.

———, *Early Mādhyamika in India and China*. Madison, Wis.: University of Wisconsin Press, 1967. Read pp. 21–70.

———, "The Sūtra of Vimalakīrti's Preaching." Manuscript submitted to Columbia University Press. Translation from the most popular Chinese version, with introduction and commentary.

Streng, Frederick J., *Emptiness: A Study in Religious Meaning*. Abingdon Press, 1967. A study of Nāgārjuna and his vision with respect to the relation between religious awareness and symbolic expression. Contains complete translations of Nāgārjuna's two chief works.

The Bodhisattva Path

Dayal, Har, *The Bodhisattva Doctrine in Buddhist Sanskrit Literature*. London: Kegan Paul, 1932.

Guenther, Herbert V., trans., *The Jewel Ornament of Liberation*, by Sgam-po-pa. London: Rider, 1959. An excellent Tibetan manual of the Bodhisattva Course. Hard to read because the translator uses nonstandard equivalents for technical terms.

Robinson, Richard H., "The Religion of the Householder Bodhisattva," in *Bhāratī*, Banaras, 1966, pp. 31–55.

The Celestial Bodhisattvas

Inde Classique No. 2336–39.

Lamotte, Étienne, *Histoire du Bouddhisme Indien*. Louvain: Publications Universitaires, 1958. Great scholar, great book. Maitreya, pp. 775–788.

———, "Mañjuśrī," *T'oung Pao*, XLVIII (1960), pp. 1–96.

Warren, *op. cit.*, pp. 480–486.

The Celestial Buddhas

"Akṣobhya," *EB*, vol. 3, pp. 363*b*–368*a*.

"Amita," *EB*, vol. 3, pp. 434*a*–463*b*.

Kern, H., trans., *The Saddharma-puṇḍarīka or the Lotus of the True Law*, in *SBE*, vol. 21. Oxford: Clarendon, 1909. An obsolete masterpiece. The only complete English translation available.

Müller, F. Max, trans., (1) *The Larger Sukhāvatī-vyūha,* in *SBE,* vol. 49, pp. 1–72, (2) *The Smaller Sukhāvatī-vyūha,* in *SBE,* vol. 49, pp. 89–103.

The Shinshu Seiten ("The Holy Scripture of Shinshu"), compiled and published by the Honpa Hongwanji Mission of Hawaii, Honolulu, 1955. The three chief Pure Land Sūtras translated from the standard Chinese versions, plus other texts from Chinese and Japanese.

Takakusu, J., trans., *The Amitāyur-dhyāna-sūtra,* in *SBE,* vol. 49, pp. 161–201.

The Doctrine of Mind-Only

Chatterjee, Ashok Kumar, *The Yogācāra Idealism.* Banaras Hindu University Press, 1962. A weak book, but the only one in English.

Conze, *Thought,* pp. 250–260.

Fukaura, Seibun, "Ālaya-vijñāna," *EB,* vol. 3, pp. 382*b*–388*b*.

Lamotte, Étienne, *La Somme du Grand Véhicule d'Asaṅga* (Mahāyānasaṃgraha). Tome II traduction et commentaire. Louvain, Muséon, 1938. A basic manual of Vijñānavāda.

Poussin, Louis de La Vallée, *La Siddhi de Hiuen-tsang* (hereafter referred to as *Siddhi*). Paris: Geuthner, 1928–1948. Translation of Hsüan-tsang's *Ch'eng-wei-shih-lun,* a synthetic commentary on the *Thirty Verses* of Vasubandhu.

Rahula, Walpola, "Asaṅga," *EB* II, vol. 113*b*–146*b*.

Robinson, *Classical Indian Philosophy,* pp. 79–85.

Suzuki, D. T., trans., *The Laṅkāvatāra Sūtra.* London: Kegan Paul, 1932 and 1956.

———, *Studies in the Laṅkāvatāra Sūtra.* London: Routledge, 1930. A fine treatment of the Sūtra's version of Yogācāra.

The Vajrayāna

Guenther, Herbert V., *The Life and Teaching of Nāropa.* Oxford University Press, 1963. Study of a great Tantric adept.

Lessing, Ferdinand, and Wayman, Alex, trans., *Fundamentals of the Buddhist Tantras,* by Mkhas-grub-rje. The Hague: Mouton, 1968. Useful translation of a schoolman's marginalia on Tsongkhapa's Tantric writings.

Snellgrove, David L., *The Hevajra Tantra.* Part I, Introduction and Translation. London: Oxford University Press, 1959. The only complete Tantra available in English. Readable and well-informed introduction.

———, "The Tantras," in Conze, *Texts,* pp. 220–268.

The Extinction of Buddhism in India

Conze, Edward, *A Short History of Buddhism.* Bombay: Chetana, 1960. A fine synoptic history. Collapse of Indian Buddhism, pp. 84–88.

CHAPTER 4

General on China

Ch'en, Kenneth, *Buddhism in China, A Historical Survey.* Princeton, 1964. Has at least something on everything. Excellent on historical facts, weak on doctrine and interpretation, extensive bibliography.

de Bary, Wm. Theodore, ed., *Sources of Chinese Tradition.* Columbia University

Press, 1960. Pages 306–408 contain Chinese Buddhist texts, well chosen and well translated by Leon Hurvitz.

Robinson, Richard H., *Chinese Buddhist Verse* (hereafter referred to as *Verse*). London: John Murray, 1955. Didactic and liturgical hymns from the Chinese Canon.

Takakusu, Junjiro, *The Essentials of Buddhist Philosophy*. Honolulu, 1947. Data-rich but opaque textbook material on the Sino-Japanese sects.

Thompson, Laurence G., *Chinese Religion: An Introduction*. "Religious Life of Man" series, Dickenson, 1969. Places Buddhism within the total panorama of Chinese religiosity.

Waley, Arthur, "Texts from China and Japan," in Conze, *Texts*, pp. 269–306. Choice morsels that Waley happened to like.

Wright, Arthur F., *Buddhism in Chinese History*. Stanford University Press, 1959. Readable, strong on history, weak on doctrine. See review by Richard H. Robinson, *Journal of the American Oriental Society*, vol. 79 (1959), pp. 311–318.

First to Sixth Centuries

Robinson, *Early Mādhyamika*. Concerns the years around 400 A.D., the Buddho-Taoists, and the first serious Chinese attempt to master an Indian treatise system.

Zürcher, Erik, *The Buddhist Conquest of China*. Leiden: Brill, 1959. Social and doctrinal history till 400 A.D. A great book, perspicacious on all facets of the subject.

T'ien-t'ai

de Bary, *op. cit.*, pp. 349–368.

Hurvitz, Leon, *Chih-i (538–597): An Introduction to the Life and Ideas of a Chinese Buddhist Monk*. Mélanges Chinois et Bouddhiques, XII, Bruges (Belgique), 1963. The only good book in English on T'ien-t'ai.

Takakusu, *op. cit.*, pp. 126–141.

San-lun

de Bary, *op. cit.*, pp. 333–343.

Takakusu, *op. cit.*, pp. 96–107.

Fa-hsiang

de Bary, *op. cit.*, pp. 343–349.

Poussin, La Vallée, *Siddhi*.

Takakusu, *op. cit.*, pp. 80–95.

Waley, Arthur, *The Real Tripitaka*. London: Allen & Unwin, 1952. Scholarly popular book on Hsüan-tsang.

Hua-yen

Kao Kuan-ju, "Avataṃsaka Sūtra," *EB II*, vol. 3, pp. 435*a*–446*a*.

Suzuki, D. T., *Essays in Zen Buddhism*, Third Series. London: Rider, 1953. Zen and the Gaṇḍavyūha, 21–214; the best treatment of Hua-yen in English so far.

Takakusu, *op. cit.*, pp. 108–125.

Pure Land

de Bary, *op. cit.*, pp. 374–386.

Robinson, *Verse*, pp. 41–45, 64–74. The Pure Land liturgical hymns.

Shinshu Seiten, pp. 109–157 from the masters' treatises; pp. 327–338 notes on the masters.

Ch'an

Dumoulin, Heinrich, *A History of Zen Buddhism.* New York: Pantheon, 1963. Readable and scholarly, though the author's interpretations sometimes depend on Catholic apologetic concepts.

Kapleau, Philip, *The Three Pillars of Zen.* Beacon paperback, 1967. How Zen is practiced in modern Japan. Lectures by Zen masters, interviews, letters, testimonials. A lotus among the thistles of writings by Western Zen enthusiasts.

Luk, Charles, *Ch'an and Zen Teaching.* London: Rider, Series I, 1960; Series II, 1961; Series III, 1962. Sloppy translations of many important texts otherwise not accessible. See review by Richard H. Robinson, *Journal of Asian Studies,* XXI, 3 (1962), 368.

Suzuki, D. T., *Essays in Zen Buddhism.* First Series, Rider 1950, Second Series, Rider 1949. A treasury of information and insights by the man who made "Zen" an English word.

Welch, Holmes, *The Practice of Chinese Buddhism.* Harvard, 1967. Based on interviews with refugee Ch'an monks. Readable, scholarly, reliable. The best book on any regional variant of modern Buddhist monastic life.

Yampolsky, Philip, *The Platform Sutra of the Sixth Patriarch.* Columbia University Press, 1967. Translation, introduction, notes. The best scholarly treatment in English of this major scripture.

Modern China

Welch, Holmes, *The Buddhist Revival in China.* Harvard, 1968. Readable and authoritative.

Japan

Anesaki, Masaharu, *Nichiren, the Buddhist Prophet.* Harvard, 1916. A fine book on a fascinating personality.

de Bary, Wm. Theodore, ed., *Sources of the Japanese Tradition.* Columbia University Press, 1958. Essayettes and translations of Buddhist texts, pp. 93–110, 116–175, 190–266. Basic and excellent.

Dumoulin, *op. cit.,* pp. 137–268. The best part of the book.

Earhart, H. Byron, *Japanese Religion.* "Religious Life of Man" series, Dickenson, 1969. Treats Buddhism as a major strand in the over-all complex of Japanese religion. The best thing to read next.

Eliot, Charles, *Japanese Buddhism.* London, 1935 and 1959. A great book in its day. Obsolete but not superseded.

Kitagawa, Joseph M., *Religion in Japanese History.* Columbia University Press, 1966. Up-to-date, well informed and informative.

Renondeau, G., *Le Bouddhisme Japonais—Textes fondamentaux de quatre grands moines de Kamakura.* Paris: Albin Michel, 1965.

Shinshu Seiten, pp. 157–315. Writings of the Japanese Pure Land masters.

Suzuki, D. T., *Zen and Japanese Culture.* New York: Pantheon, 1959.

Southeast Asia

Byles, Marie M., *Journey into Burmese Silence*. London: Allen & Unwin, 1962. A plucky Australian lady in Burmese meditation centers. Informative about Burma and its religion, as well as about what happens when one meditates.

Cabaton, Antoine, "Cambodia," *ERE,* vol. 3, pp. 155*a*–167*a*. An over-all picture of Cambodian religious life.

Damais, Louis-Charles, "Le Bouddhisme en Indonésie," in *Présence du Bouddhisme,* pp. 813–824.

Davids, T. W. Rhys, "Ceylon Buddhism," *ERE,* vol. 3, pp. 331*a*–334*b*.

King, Winston L., *A Thousand Lives Away*. Harvard, 1964. A perceptive outsider assesses the state of Theravāda thought and values in contemporary Burma.

Rāhula, Walpola, *History of Buddhism in Ceylon*. Colombo: Gunasena, 1956. History and culture in the classical period, well described by a scholarly bhikṣu.

Scott, James George, "Burma and Assam (Buddhism in)," *ERE,* vol. 3, pp. 27*b*–43*b*.

Spiro, Melford E., *Burmese Supernaturalism*. Prentice-Hall, 1967. An anthropologist looks at the total religious system of the Burmese. See especially "Supernaturalism and Buddhism," pp. 246–280. Good up-to-date bibliography.

Wells, Kenneth E., *Thai Buddhism, Its Rites and Activities*. Bangkok: Christian Bookstore, 1960. A straight description of ceremonies, liturgies, and festivals.

Yoe, Shway (pseudonym of James George Scott), *The Burman, His Life and Notions*. London: Macmillan, 1896. Now in paperback. A sympathetic and informative classic.

Tibet

Evans-Wentz, W. Y., *The Tibetan Book of the Dead*. Oxford University Press, 3d ed., 1960.

———, *Tibetan Yoga and Secret Doctrines*. Oxford University Press, 2d ed., 1960.

———, *Tibet's Great Yogi Milarepa*. Oxford University Press, 2d ed., 1951.

Evans-Wentz is a Theosophist who worked with a bilingual Tibetan to produce translations that are readable, and notes that are often inane.

Guenther, Herbert V., *Tibetan Buddhism without Mystification*. Leiden: Brill, 1966. Translation of four eighteenth-century Gelukpa tracts, with introduction and notes.

Hoffmann, Helmut, *The Religions of Tibet*. London: Allen & Unwin, 1961. A standard work. Weak on doctrine.

Snellgrove, David and Hugh Richardson, *A Cultural History of Tibet*. New York: Praeger, 1968. Readable and authoritative. Gives a prominent place to religion. Good bibliography and maps.

AN OVERVIEW OF THE BUDDHIST SCRIPTURES

A. The Pali Canon: The *Tipiṭaka* ("Three Baskets")

See Thomas, *Thought,* pp. 265–276, and *Inde Classique* No. 1947–1979.

I *Vinaya-piṭaka* ("Basket of Discipline")

1. *Sutta-vibhaṅga* ("Division of Rules")—the rules of the Pātimokkha code with explanations and commentary.

(a) *Mahāvibhaṅga* ("Great Division")—the 227 rules for monks.
(b) *Bhikkhunī-vibhaṅga* ("Division Concerning Nuns")

2. *Khandhaka* ("Sections")
   (a) *Mahāvagga* ("Great Group")—rules for ordination, observance day, rainy-season retreat, clothing, food, medicine, and procedures of the Saṅgha.
   (b) *Cullavagga* ("Small Group")—judicial rules, miscellaneous rules, ordination and instruction of nuns, history of the First and Second Councils.
3. *Parivāra* ("The Accessory")—summaries and classifications of the rules. This is a late supplement.

II *Sutta-piṭaka,* ("Basket of Discourses")

1. *Dīgha-nikāya* ("Collection of Long Discourses")—34 suttas.
2. *Majjhima-nikāya* ("Collection of Medium Discourses")—152 suttas.
3. *Saṃyutta-nikāya* ("Collection of Connected Discourses")—56 groups of suttas.
4. *Aṅguttara-nikāya* ("Collection of Item-more Discourses")—over 2300 suttas.
5. *Khuddaka-nikāya* ("Collection of Little Texts")
   (a) *Khuddaka-pāṭha* ("Little Readings")—a breviary.
   (b) *Dhammapada* ("Verses on Dharma")—423 verses in 26 chapters.
   (c) *Udāna* ("Utterances")—80 exalted pronouncements of the Buddha, with circumstantial tales.
   (d) *Itivuttaka* ("Thus-saids")—112 short suttas.
   (e) *Sutta-nipāta* ("Collection of Suttas")—short suttas, mostly in verse of high poetic quality.
   (f) *Vimāna-vatthu* ("Tales of Heavenly Mansions")—gods tell the deeds that earned them celestial rebirths.
   (g) *Peta-vatthu* ("Tales of Ghosts")—how various persons attained that unfortunate rebirth.
   (h) *Thera-gāthā* ("Verses of the Elders")—stanzas attributed to 264 personal disciples of the Buddha.
   (i) *Therī-gāthā* ("Verses of the Eldresses")—stanzas attributed to about 100 lady disciples of the Buddha.
   (j) *Jātaka* ("Lives")—tales ostensibly reporting the former lives of Śākyamuni. The verses in each tale are supposed to have been uttered by the Buddha, and so are considered canonical; but the 547 tales themselves are extracanonical.
   (k) *Niddesa* ("Exposition")—verbal notes to part of the Sutta-nipāta. The Niddesa is second or third century A.D.
   (l) *Paṭisambhidā-magga* ("The Way of Analysis")—Abhidharma-style treatment of some doctrinal topics.
   (m) *Apadāna* ("Stories")—lives and former lives of the saints.
   (n) *Buddhavaṃsa* ("Lineage of the Buddhas")—lives of 24 previous Buddhas, of Śākyamuni, and of Maitreya, presented as being told by Śākyamuni.
   (o) *Cariyā-piṭaka* ("Basket on Conduct")—verse retellings of Jātakas illustrating the Bodhisattva's practice of the perfections.

III *Abhidhamma-piṭaka* ("Basket of Scholasticism")

1. *Dhamma-saṅgani* ("Enumeration of Dharmas")
2. *Vibhaṅga* ("Divisions")—more on sets of dharmas.
3. *Dhātu-kathā* ("Discussion of Elements")
4. *Puggala-paññatti* ("Designation of Persons")—classifies people according to their spiritual traits and stages.
5. *Kathā-vatthu* ("Subjects of Discussion")—arguments about theses in dispute among the Hīnayāna schools.
6. *Yamaka* ("The Pairs")—arranged in pairs of questions, deals with the basic sets of categories.
7. *Paṭṭhāna* ("Activations")—24 kinds of causal relation.

B. The Chinese Canon: The *Ta-ts'ang-ching* ("Great Scripture-Store")

See Ch'en, pp. 365–378, and *Inde Classique,* No. 2107–2162.

The first printed edition was produced in Szechuan, in 972–983 A.D. It consisted of 1,076 texts in 480 cases. The standard modern edition is the *Taishō Shinshū Daizōkyō* (Ta-ts'ang-ching newly edited in the Taishō reign-period). It was published in Tokyo, 1924–1929, and consists of 55 Western-style volumes containing 2184 texts. A supplement consists of 45 volumes. The following analysis is of the Taishō edition.

I *Āgama* Section, vol. 1–2, 151 texts. Contains the Long, Medium, Mixed (= Connected) and Item-more Āgamas, plus some individual texts corresponding to parts of the Pali Khuddaka.

II Story Section, vol. 3–4, 68 texts. *Jātakas,* lives of various Buddhas, fables, and parables.

III *Prajñā-pāramitā* Section, vol. 5–8, 42 texts.

IV *Saddharma-puṇḍarīka* Section, vol. 9, 16 texts. Three complete versions of the Lotus Sūtra, plus some doctrinally cognate Sūtras.

V *Avataṃsaka* Section, vol. 9–10, 31 texts.

VI *Ratnakūṭa* Section, vol. 11–12, 64 texts. A set of 49 Mahāyāna Sūtras, some in more than one translation.

VII *Mahāparinirvāṇa* Section, vol. 12, 23 texts. The Mahāyāna version of Śākyamuni's last days and words.

VIII Great Assembly Section, vol. 13, 28 texts. A collection beginning with the Great Assembly Sūtra, which is itself a suite of Mahāyāna Sūtras.

IX Sūtra-collection Section, vol. 14–17, 423 texts. A miscellany of Sūtras, mostly Mahāyāna.

X Tantra Section, vol. 18–21, 572 texts. Vajrayāna Sūtras, Tantras, ritual manuals, and spells.

XI Vinaya Section, vol. 22–24, 86 texts. Vinayas of the Mahīśāsakas, Mahāsaṅghikas, Dharmaguptakas, Sarvāstivādins, and Mūla-sarvāstivādins. Also some texts on the Bodhisattva discipline.

XII Commentaries on Sūtras, vol. 24–26, 31 texts—on Āgamas and on Mahāyāna Sūtras, by Indian authors.

XIII Abhidharma Section, vol. 26–29, 28 texts. Scholastic treatises of the Sarvāstivādins, Dharmaguptakas, and Sautrāntikas.

XIV Mādhyamika Section, vol. 30, 15 texts.

XV Yogācāra Section, vol. 30–31, 49 texts.

XVI Collection of Treatises, vol. 32, 65 texts. Works on logic, anthologies from the Sūtras, and sundry treatises.
XVII Commentaries on the Sūtras, vol. 33–39, by Chinese authors.
XVIII Commentaries on the Vinaya, vol. 40, by Chinese authors.
XIX Commentaries on the Śāstras, vol. 40–44, by Chinese authors.
XX Chinese Sectarian Writings, vol. 44–48.
XXI History and Biography, vol. 49–52, 95 texts.
XXII Encyclopedias and Dictionaries, vol. 53–54, 16 texts.
XXIII Non-Buddhist Doctrines, vol. 54, 8 texts. Sāṃkhya, Vaiśeṣika, Manichean, and Nestorian Christian writings.
XXIV Catalogs, vol. 55, 40 texts. Successive catalogs of the Canon beginning with that of Seng-yu published in 515 A.D.

C. The Tibetan Canon

See *Inde Classique,* Nos. 2033–2044, and Kenneth Ch'en, "The Tibetan Tripiṭaka," *Harvard Journal of Asian Studies* 9 (1945–47), pp. 53–62.

I *Bka'-'gyur* (*Kanjur*) ("Translation of Buddha-word") The number of volumes and order of sections differs slightly from edition to edition. The following is according to the Snar-thang (Narthang) version.
1. *Vinaya,* 13 vols.
2. *Prajñā-pāramitā,* 21 vols.
3. *Avataṃsaka,* 6 vols.
4. *Ratnakūṭa,* 6 vols. A set of 49 Mahāyāna Sūtras.
5. *Sūtra,* 30 vol., 270 texts, three-quarters Mahāyāna Sūtras and one-quarter Hīnayāna ones.
6. *Tantra,* 22 vol., over 300 texts.

II *Bstan-'gyur* (*Tenjur*) ("Translation of Teachings") In the Peking edition, this consists of 224 volumes and 3626 texts, divided into:
1. *Stotras* (hymns of praise), 1 vol., 64 texts.
2. *Commentaries on Tantras,* 86 vols., 3055 texts.
3. *Commentaries on Sūtras,* 137 vols., 567 texts.
   (a) *Prajñā-pāramitā* commentaries, 16 vols.
   (b) *Mādhyamika* treatises, 17 vols.
   (c) *Yogācāra* treatises, 29 vols.
   (d) *Abhidharma,* 8 vols.
   (e) Miscellaneous, 4 vols.
   (f) *Vinaya* Commentaries, 16 vols.
   (g) Tales and dramas, 4 vols.
   (h) Technical treatises: logic (21 vols.), grammar (1 vol.), lexicography and poetics (1 vol.), medicine (5 vols.), chemistry and sundry (1 vol.), supplement (old and recent translations, indices; 14 vols.).

Index